ABOUT THE AUTHOR

James Bragg has been a full-time consumer advocate for over 20 years as the day-to-day, hands-on founder-manager of Fighting Chance.com, a national information service that's helped over 125,000 consumers buy or lease a new vehicle. Much of his knowledge has come from his personal contacts with tens of thousands of those customers.

His objective has always been to uncover information and develop negotiating strategies that help consumers get the best deal available, often revealing truths no other information source is providing. His penetrating, "outside-the-box" analysis and recommendations fly in the face of over 30 years of conventional wisdom about how to buy a new car.

He's the author of the *Car Buyer's and Leaser's Negotiating Bible*, a Random House publication that notched 65,000 sales over four editions. He now owns the rights to the book and plans to update it.

His business background is rich and varied. He's been a Procter & Gamble Brand Manager and a Hunt-Wesson Foods New Products Director, and he's managed the national corporate and regional dealer advertising programs for an auto brand.

Mr. Bragg is a graduate of Phillips Academy (Andover), Yale University (Phi Beta Kappa) and the Harvard Business School.

D1018617

TABLE OF CONTENTS

Preface

1. Why I Wrote This Book   1
No one was telling consumers the truth. Somebody had to. After 15+ years uncovering it, I knew if I didn't do it, no one would.

2. Question authority.   4
Why we shouldn't trust everything those online "experts" tell us.

3. George Will was right.   8
How we short-circuit our connection with reality when we send our common sense on an extended vacation.

4. What if the store were ours?   11
Probing how you and I would act if our skins were in the game.

5. My vine has 125,000 grapes.   14
How my customers' transaction reports cast serious doubt on what Consumer Reports and those auto-pricing websites are telling us.

6. The way it is . . is not the way it was.   21
How the information you're getting about "dealer incentives" is so out-of-touch with today's reality, it should be wearing bell-bottoms in the Smithsonian.

7. "Loose lips sink ships."   26
The wealth of "inside information" my customers pick up from dealer personnel during the purchase process paints a revealing behind-the-scenes picture that points to just one conclusion.

8. Hiding (in plain sight)   36
Sometimes the answer to a puzzling question is right under your nose. Once I got a good sniff, I was on that scent like a mad dog on a wounded squirrel.

9. Eureka!   39
How a few old books, some archeological number digging and a "cold case" analysis uncovered the sea change in the invoice-retail price relationship that began in 1995 and continues today, an eye-opening bombshell the big auto-info players seem to have missed.

Letting The Cat Out Of The Bag

How The Auto Industry "Redesigned" The Dealer Invoice Price When The Internet Arrived

James Bragg

Second Edition

10. $ilence is golden. 51
Why I'm convinced the big auto-pricing websites, including Consumer Reports, which were given living proof of this "redesign" in November 2012, haven't enlightened you on the subject.

11. The dealer is not your enemy. 63
The bum rap dealers get. How they've improved their act dramatically. And why you should cut them some slack.

12. The cards have been dealt. 66
The "truth cards" are in your hand. It's time to review what you've learned and what you should do with this knowledge the next time you're new-car shopping — including what your objective should be and the best way to achieve it.

Epilogue 70
I'm just planting the seeds. To grow this forest of truth, these seedlings must be planted more broadly. I need your help to make that happen.

"The Exhibit" 72
The data "bombshell" that neuters all the information and negotiating advice you're being fed on and off the Internet.

Words Truth Seekers Live By 85
Almost all of which are relevant to the subject of this book.

PREFACE

Automakers redesign their vehicles about every five or six years. They shine their headlights brightly on those new-and-improved beauties to spread the word to every nook and cranny in America.

But no headlights have been cast on the jaw-dropping "total redesign" of the automaker-dealer financial relationship that began in the mid-1990s and has continued, year after year, ever since.

This book is the stand-in for those headlights that went AWOL when they should have been trained on that seismic shift in the way dealers are compensated. It's about why and how that "redesign" was done and how it changes what you should do to shop smart for a new car.

It's also a critique of those well-known sources of new-car pricing and negotiating advice, the "experts" we would have expected to uncover and reveal this game-changing information to us over a decade ago, but seem to have either missed it or chosen to ignore it.

In sharp contrast to those trusted sources, this book will open your eyes to the pivotal fact about the new-car business that's been hidden from you for almost twenty years.

It should convince you to ignore everything you're being told about the smart way to buy a new vehicle on all those "expert" websites.

"The truth is incontrovertible. Malice may attack it. Ignorance may deride it, but in the end, there it is."

— Winston Churchill

*"I never did give anybody hell.
I just told the truth, and they
thought it was hell."*

— **Harry Truman**

Ditto!

Spike

"It ain't what you don't know that gets you into trouble. It's what you know for sure that just ain't so."

— Mark Twain

1

Why I Wrote This Book

I never thought I'd be writing a book that could change how consumers understand and approach the dreaded process of buying or leasing a new vehicle. But after twenty years as perhaps the country's only full-time consumer advocate for new-car shoppers, I realized that if I didn't write it, no one would.

I've long suspected that the conventional wisdom about the financial relationship between automakers and their dealers was several gas stops short of the whole truth. I was running into so many anomalies to that wisdom that I felt there had to be a "missing link" in the information chain. If I was right, all the negotiating advice the Internet "experts" were dispensing based on that information was both misleading and a threat to consumers' bank balances.

This book is about the quest to find that link and confirm its existence by uncovering the core facts needed to expose the whole truth.

Initially, my skepticism was based on plain old common sense, which almost shouted at me that the basic assumption behind the information and advice we were getting was whacko! It just couldn't be true about any retail business.

But nobody's "gut feeling" ever proved anything. I had to dig out the facts that would confirm that what was in my gut wasn't just indigestion.

I was probably in a unique position to tackle this.

• I've been a consumer advocate for new-vehicle shoppers since before the Dead Sea got sick.

• As the hands-on owner-operator of Fighting Chance.com, a unique, personally-accessible information service founded in 1992, I've logged over 60,000 hours focused on one subject: the consumer's smart purchase and lease of new vehicles.

• And since I get no revenue from the automobile business, I have no conflict-of-interest issues.

I have never been an "insider" in that business. But I managed an auto brand's advertising campaigns for several years.

I've also learned a lot from people I've met in the auto business, some of whose advertising accounts I've "pitched" over the years.

Most important, I've had a 20-year personal relationship with tens of thousands of "consumer spies," car-shopping customers who add to my expanding knowledge of the subject every working day.

I've helped over 125,000 consumers negotiate the best deals available. Some of the most revealing insights have come from their post-purchase phone calls and transaction reports. They've provided the building blocks that have helped piece together a behind-the-scenes picture of how the money side of the business really works today — a picture often aided by comments made by loose-lipped dealer personnel.

Some will claim that I wrote this book as a commercial for Fighting Chance. That's not true. It will remain what it's been for 20+ years: an information service small enough to enable us to talk to our customers, answer their questions and learn from their experiences. We're selling little pieces of ourselves, and we can talk to only a limited number of new-vehicle shoppers each day.

I'm a healthy 78-year-old who quit playing baseball (not that wimpy game of softball) competitively with men in their 30s and 40s when I was 72. I have no interest in "retirement." (I hate golf.) I'm on a mission to spread the truth broadly, a consumer advocate-turned-activist who's not going away anytime soon. I don't invent the news. I just dig it out and report it when it's clear that no one else will.

I am not "anti-dealer." (You'll understand this in the chapter titled "The Dealer Is Not Your Enemy.") But I am tenaciously "pro-consumer" and "pro-truth" — *the whole truth.* When no one else is telling it, I will.

Twelve to thirteen million Americans buy or lease a new car every day. I believe they're all entitled to that truth when they're making their second most expensive purchase. But they're not getting it from those long-trusted, "expert" new-car information websites.

It took over a decade of slowly mounting evidence to paint a complete, credible picture of *the whole truth.* The picture is fact-based and leads to a single logical conclusion.

In essence, this book presents the strong opinions I've come to, built on a rational, step-by-step analysis that: (1) starts with a solid base of common sense about consumers and business in general, (2) adds a mountain of anecdotal evidence from over 20 years of conversations with my customers and their transaction reports, (3) exposes in stark detail the incontrovertible, year-by-year total reconstruction of the automaker-dealer financial relationship and (4) finishes with my assessment of the questionable value to consumers of the car-buying information and negotiating advice on the Internet.

At USA TODAY's invitation, I participated in a November 27, 2012 open and candid roundtable discussion on *"whether online car shopping and information services are believable and are relevant in today's market."* At the meeting I distributed an exhibit with the undeniable evidence of that "missing link" to senior executives of Consumer Reports, Kelley Blue Book, Edmunds, TrueCar and Cars.com. (You'll find it starting on page 72 of this book.) All the participants left with that exhibit.

The newspaper's December 7, 2012 article on that meeting seemed to echo my conclusion. The headline: "Surprising tips for car shopping in the Internet age." Followed by: "While sharp-minded buyers are likely to feel almost smug nowadays, armed with more inside information than ever, it can be incomplete and misleading." (Google "USA TODAY Automotive Roundtable" to read the online version of that piece.)

The discovery process was like peeling an onion, layer by layer, to get to the truth at its core. I'd say it will be eye-opening, but . . well, . . onions and eyes are not the most comfortable metaphor companions.

One of my heroes is the late Andy Rooney, the legendary weekly commentator on *60 Minutes* who died at 92, one month after his final regular appearance. My favorite Rooney quote is, "I believe that if all the truth were known about everything in the world, it would be a better place to live."

With a tip of the cap to Andy, let's start peeling that onion.

James Bragg

"No statement should be believed just because it was made by an authority. "

— Robert A. Heinlein
Science fiction writer (1907-1988)

2

Question authority.

We're all a tad gullible. If there's something we know little about, we tend to believe what we're told by those who appear to be more knowledgeable. A body of "conventional wisdom" develops on the subject that is widely communicated by "authoritative sources" that we come to trust. They tell us what they believe is the truth, and we accept it at face value.

But what's the basis for their belief? Is it logical? Accurate? Fact-centered? Current? What if the answer to those questions was "yes" for many years, but then the underlying facts changed dramatically, invalidating their information and advice? If they failed to bring their position into synch with the new reality, would that mean they were lying to us, or "conning" us?

Not necessarily. It might simply mean they were behind the curve of events and hadn't caught up with the new paradigm on the subject. You can't be telling a lie if you don't know the truth.

But alternatively, it might mean that they had a vested interest in the status quo and found the newly revealed truth disruptive, even threatening.

Whenever a new way of thinking obsoletes an old way, there are winners and losers.

For centuries, the world's most respected thinkers were convinced that the earth was flat, so that became the conventional wisdom. Those ancient wise men, priests and philosophers who championed the flat-earth position were feted and revered by their adoring believers. They had a good thing going.

Then one day in 1519 it was gone, when Ferdinand Magellan woke up and said, "Those guys are whacko! That flat-earth gibberish doesn't make sense. If the earth were flat, all the water in the ocean would fall off the edge, right? But if it does, where does it go, and why don't the oceans dry up? I've gotta get a big stash of cash from King Charlie and go find out." He was the first to circumnavigate the globe. And his discovery wiped out several centuries of conventional wisdom and put a few thousand wise guys on the unemployment line.

Those whackos have their modern counterparts. The Flat Earth Society lives and breathes today, a ragged collection of 3,000 mentally-challenged folks who hold that "humanity lives on a disc, with the North Pole at its center and a 150-foot high wall of ice at the outer edge." (Check them out on Wikipedia for a few grins.)

But I digress, for which I apologize and return to the business at hand . . . .

For several decades, consumers have looked to authoritative sources they trust, on and off the Internet, for information and advice on how to navigate a purchase process they detest (buying a new car) and end up feeling good about the result.

Over those decades, a body of "conventional wisdom" developed on the subject that's still in general use today. Its core element is *the dealer invoice price*," which has become the basis on which consumers gauge the quality of the deal they've struck. If the selling price they get is near to or below that number, most folks feel they've done reasonably well.

That's because they think the dealer invoice is a good estimate of the dealer's real cost. That's what they've been led to believe over the years by those authoritative sources they trust. And all those "experts" have been singing from the same page of the hymn book, using the invoice price as the foundation for their information and advice.

Alternate "experts" figure their net invoice numbers slightly differently.

• Some add an estimate of the automaker's mandatory regional group advertising charge.

• Some subtract "holdback" — money in the invoice price that's returned to dealers after the sale, typically 1% to 3% of the invoice or sticker price.

Some auto info websites may indicate that all new vehicles have holdback, perhaps even showing estimated dollar amounts for each model. But holdback is on its way to extinction. Some brands have already eliminated it. Audi, BMW and Land Rover haven't had it in years. Lexus deep-sixed it in February 2012, and Lincoln followed suit later that year. Mercedes dumped it in April 2013. Those dollars remain in the dealer invoice price, but that money goes to other, secret dealer incentive programs, so car shoppers can no longer use it as a "bargaining chip.".

I believe Jaguar, Mini and Scion also have no holdback. I expect more automakers to dump it in the next several years, using those dollars to reward dealers in other ways, many of which may have no relation to sales (e.g., covering the cost of free "loaner cars" to service customers). Slowly but steadily, holdback is riding off into the sunset.

However the invoice prices are figured, the implicit message consumers get from those "authorities" is that those numbers are their "expert" estimates of *the true dealer cost*. (Fighting Chance customers are typically educated, sophisticated adults, but most of them come to me believing that.)

That amount, those trusted sources have claimed or implied over the years, is the information we need to "negotiate the amount of profit" the dealer will make on the sale. It's also typically the base number they use as they go through the rationale for both the target prices and the negotiating tactics they recommend.

Since we're all babes in the woods on this subject, this sounds to us like the "inside skinny," so we've swallowed it — hook, line and sinker.

Problem is, the dealer invoice price, even after subtracting holdback dollars and any of the less common vehicle-specific dealer cash incentives, is not a true dealer cost item today. Instead, it's an imposter posing as the genuine article, a fictional smokescreen developed to hide the reality. As a result, those online "target prices" that are based on that imposter will never make dealers unhappy. And they typically won't be the best prices available in your market.

A bevy of auto-info website "authorities" can tell us "what a dealer paid" for any new car on his lot. But the implicit assumption that what he paid *initially* is what he *ends up* paying (or even close to it) is at odds with both common sense and the reality of today's financial relationship between automakers and their dealers.

Given their decades of experience with new-car pricing and their day-to-day contact with its frequent changes, wouldn't you think that someone at one or two of those "authorities" would have had enough curiosity to notice the dramatic "redesign" of that financial relationship as it unfolded right before their eyes, year after year, for over 18 years?

Isn't that a colossal oversight by organizations known as reliable sources of new-car pricing?

So how credible are those "authorities" on this subject? Consumers perceive the pricing they provide as a real dealer cost item. But that perception is based on an implicit assumption about the factory-dealer financial relationship that hasn't been true for over 18 years. What does that say about the competence and/or willingness of those "authorities" to dig out and report the truth?

And if many of those "authorities" were handed the stone-cold proof of the total reconstruction of that relationship late in 2012, but have ignored it and made no change in the information and advice they're giving you when you're making your second most expensive purchase, what does that say about the strength of their commitment to help you win?

In my view, that's like handing us a tattered red cape, giving us a rubber sword, opening the arena door and introducing us to the angry bull. (Guess who gets skewered in that contest.)

Yes, Andy, the world would be a better place if all the truth were known about everything.

As a corollary, consumers would be able to negotiate better new-vehicle prices if they knew the truth about how new-car dealers are compensated for their sales.

Isn't it about time someone let that cat out of the bag and illustrated convincingly why "no statement should be believed just because it was made by an authority?"

"This is an age in which one cannot find common sense without a search warrant."

— George Will
American Journalist & Author

3 (Onion layer #1)

George Will was right.

Let's face it. We all dread the task of buying or leasing a new car. We'd rather take a long walk off a short pier. Or suffer through a root canal procedure. That makes this a situation where the stars are perfectly aligned to make smart people do dumb things.

There's a mountain of car-buying information and advice on the Internet. We feel terribly mismatched in that process, so we spend hours climbing that mountain, hoping to find a way to level the playing field.

But somewhere along the way, we abandon our common sense and start believing everything we're told there. The purpose of this chapter is to jump-start yours and give it some necessary exercise.

Common sense is typically defined as "sound and prudent judgment based on a simple perception of the situation or facts." It's the body of knowledge and experience people gain as they become adults.

The Cambridge Dictionary calls it "the basic level of practical knowledge and judgment that we all need to help us live in a reasonable and safe way."

Assuming you feel you can make "sound and prudent judgments based on a simple perception of the situation or facts," let's start exercising that ability.

• For openers, we purchase hundreds of goods and services each year for ourselves and our families — items sold on the Internet and in a gazillion retail stores.

• And there isn't a single one of those goods or services for which anyone can tell us the seller's cost.

• Yet it seems that for years we've been willing to believe that some consumer-oriented organization or new-car pricing website can tell us what a new-car dealer "really pays" for a $12,000 to $100,000+ vehicle.

Mind you, the dealership is owned by a corporation or a successful person or family with strong business acumen and a $10 million net worth, at least $5 million of which is invested in their car store. "Stupid" doesn't get anyone to $10 million. Do you think those owners would allow you and me to know the *true cost* of the cars they sell? Really?

Does that pass your common sense sniff test?

• Now ponder this: If Consumer Reports and other auto-pricing websites can give us a number close to a dealer's real cost, why are new cars the only products for which this info is available? If we can get it for cars, isn't it odd that no similar service provides it for motorcycles, boats, motor homes, tractors, private airplanes, home appliances, flat-screen TV sets, iPhones, ground beef, prescriptions, insurance policies, t-shirts, jeans, Q-Tips, etc.?

Doesn't this wave another common-sense red flag?

• Now let's examine whether the gross profit built into the widely-available new-car pricing info passes our common sense test. Those invoice prices we can readily find are accompanied by the corresponding manufacturer's suggested retail or "sticker" prices, which are posted by federal law on every new vehicle's window sticker.

A cursory look at today's invoice/retail price relationship reveals that there's not a single new car with more than a 10% difference between the invoice price and the MSRP. The manufacturers' suggested retail prices for most new vehicles carry a gross profit percentage in the range of 4% to 8%. And that's at the full sticker price! Except for the guy who just fell off the turnip truck, who pays that?

This is a fact: No retail store could operate profitably if its "cost of goods sold" were 90% of its sales. At that tiny gross margin level there wouldn't be a single store open selling anything.

Every retail store, including a new-car dealership, has substantial overhead expenses. Rent or mortgage payments, employee payroll, inventory financing charges, insurance, advertising, taxes, telephone and other office expenses. In the retail car business, that overhead expense is about 12% to 15% of total sales. To earn an acceptable profit and return on investment, a retail store's gross profit on sales before overhead must typically be in the range of 25% to 35%.

Yet we're supposed to believe an assumption that defies human logic — that the dealer invoice price (minus "holdback") is a credible estimate of what auto dealers really pay for the new vehicles they sell!

Do we abhor that purchase process so intensely that we need to believe an assertion that isn't close to being a "sound and prudent judgment based on a simple perception of the situation or facts?"

Are we really that gullible? Aren't we just conning ourselves when we accept as true information that flies in the face of our common sense?

Let's follow this line of thinking by examining how we'd act if we had some serious skins in the retail game.

"Everything is funny, as long as it's happening to somebody else."

— Will Rogers

4 (Onion layer #2)

What if the store were ours?

The purpose of this chapter is to drive the "common sense" message home by making the situation personally relevant to you and me.

But first, ponder this: Where do you think Consumer Reports and those auto-pricing websites get dealer invoice prices? From skywriters? Candy wrappers? Twitter? Cereal boxes? YouTube? Lottery tickets? Victoria's Secret catalogues?

Believe it or not, that information comes straight from the horse's mouth — the automakers that set those prices. Why are dealer invoice prices made public? I'm not omniscient, but here's my take:

Traditionally, the automakers' captive finance companies provided about 40% of new-vehicle financing. Banks had roughly the same share, and credit unions and independent finance companies accounted for the other 20%.

Those important third-party financing sources needed that information to be confident that they weren't loaning a lot more money than the vehicles were worth. So the automakers had to provide it to lending institutions, which shared it with their loan prospects. As a result, those numbers became public information anyone could access by walking into a bank. Eventually they also were published periodically in *Edmund's* and *ConsumerGuide* paperbacks, and they were available from Consumer Reports' New Car Price Service.

At an early 1980s market research luncheon meeting, I sat next to the day's keynote speaker, one of the country's most knowledgeable researchers on the retail auto business. I asked him, "What percentage of new-car shoppers walks into car stores with the dealer invoice price numbers?" His answer: "Not over 10% to 15%."

That didn't become a serious problem for dealers until the Internet exploded in the mid-1990s, when any doofus with five thumbs and a keyboard could get the invoice prices for free without leaving home. Let's inject ourselves into a scenario similar to the one faced then by car dealers.

- Assume you and I owned a successful retail store selling something reasonably expensive, like those $2,000+ flat-screen TV sets.

- Let's further assume that, like the automakers, the TV manufacturers revealed our "dealer invoice prices," and websites similar to those big auto-pricing sites made them available to anyone interested in buying what we sell.

We're not stupid. If those invoice prices were what we really paid for those flat screens — or even close to it — it wouldn't have taken us more than two minutes to call Sony, Samsung, Panasonic, JVC, Sharp, Toshiba, Sanyo and the others and scream, "We're getting killed here! If you don't find a way to compensate us that consumers can't find out about, no stores will sell your products!"

New-car dealers aren't stupid either. If those invoice prices that started showing up on those auto-pricing websites in the mid-1990s were anywhere near their real costs, wouldn't every dealer have made the same phone call? Wouldn't they have been on those automakers like ugly on a baboon?

But they weren't.

Their invoice prices have continued to be widely available, on and off the Internet, year after year. And no dealers complain.

Shouldn't that jolt us into doubting those who want us to believe that the invoice price, however they define it, is close to the bona fide *dealer cost* and recommend that we aim for target prices that are based on that number?

Wouldn't that doubt be "a sound and prudent judgment based on a simple perception of the situation or facts?"

I'll tell you a little secret. Auto dealers absolutely *love* having those invoice numbers broadcast all over the Internet! And that's because, on this subject, they know we've sent our common sense on a multi-year vacation to Dumbsville, and we're willing to believe anything we're told.

Do you believe, readers, that dealers and automakers, *the only possible sources of the real cost information*, would make it available to Consumer Reports or any other car-pricing organization if they really didn't want you to know those numbers? Does that pass your common sense sniff test? Isn't that naivety on stilts?

Well over ten years ago these common-sense considerations convinced me that dealers were receiving a very substantial amount of hidden revenue from automakers.

Clearly, there was a missing link in the factory-to-dealer revenue stream that everyone in or dependent on the auto business was hiding. I was determined to find that link, focusing on each new piece of evidence as it was uncovered over several years.

The next few chapters will take us further into that onion.

Smokey Robinson & The Miracles/1966
Gladys Knight & The Pips/1967
Marvin Gaye/1968
Creedence Clearwater Revival/1970
The California Raisins/1986
James Bragg & The Informants/1992-2013

5 (Onion layer #3)

My vine has 125,000 grapes.

In life, they shuffle those cards again every day. If we're paying attention, we should learn something from each day's deal that we can use to our benefit thereafter.

Years ago I worked with Joe Dolan, one of Bobby Kennedy's key assistants for many years. Ted Kennedy's reputation when he entered politics was less than great. One day I asked Joe, "Is Ted really smart?"

Joe told me about Bobby's passion for growing continually as an adult. He said, "Whenever I mentioned something that piqued Bobby's curiosity, he asked me how I knew that. The next day he had a book on the subject under his arm. I see the same inner drive in Ted, and I think he'll be an important contributing member of Congress." (Democrats and Republicans agree that he was one of the most accomplished legislative senators in history.)

Running a hands-on information service for twenty years and talking regularly to customers in the car-war trenches, you learn something every day that I doubt you'd ever pick up running Consumer Reports' New Car Price Service or one of those "corporate" auto-pricing websites that get millions of visitors a month. What I glean from those conversations helps me make consumers smarter about the second most expensive purchase they make.

• Let's start with the prices Fighting Chance customers report negotiating for the new vehicles they buy or lease.

Consumer Reports and those auto websites calculate their claims of the "dollars saved" using their "dealer network's" buying service by subtracting the vehicle's selling price from the full sticker price.

Does that pass your common sense test? (It flunks mine.)

Excluding those who think Taco Bell is a Mexican phone company, who pays the sticker price today?

Those sites also often count any customer rebates in effect to inflate their bogus "savings" claims.

Legally, everyone who buys a new vehicle, even Goofy, gets that cash. They sign a release authorizing the automaker to credit that money to the dealer's account as part of their down payment. If a dealer got caught forging a buyer's signature to steal that money, the state's attorney general would be on that store like a blind buzzard on road kill.

So whenever you see a "savings" claim on one of those sites, be sure to check how it was figured. If it's been figured the way most sites figure it, it's just *boomfog*.

In contrast, Fighting Chance customers report the amount they paid over or under the "total invoice price," including the destination charge, regional dealer group advertising fees and any other dealer charges (for processing, dealer prep, documentation, etc.), but before subtracting any cash incentives in effect.

To illustrate some real-world examples, I analyzed several hundred Fighting Chance customer transaction reports for some of the country's best-selling vehicles — those that you might assume would be difficult to deal on, given their popularity. That analysis yielded these results:

- 58.4% of all the prices reported were below the total dealer invoice price — often well below.
- For luxury brands, 42.4% of the prices reported were below invoice; for all others, 62.0%. For a few brands, 70% to 80% of the reports were below the invoice. And remember, that's before subtracting the effect of any cash incentives.

Here's the range of prices reported for several popular vehicles:

- **<u>One of the best-selling pickups (104 reports)</u>**
  $500-$900 over invoice (9%)
  $250-$499 over (9%)
  <u>$100-$249 over (18%)</u>
  Total Over Invoice - 36%
  Right at the Invoice Price - 11%
  $35-$200 below invoice (13%)
  $201-$400 below (11%)

$401-$700 below (12%)
$701-$1,000 below (8%)
$1,001-$1,300 below (5%)
$1,301-$1,700 below (3%)
<u>$3,100 below (1%)</u>
Total Below Invoice - 53%
Total At or Below Invoice – 64%

• <u>**One of the best-selling midsize passenger cars (168 reports)**</u>
$700-$1,250 over invoice (4%)
$300-$699 over (19%)
<u>$1-$299 over (11%)</u>
Total Over Invoice - 34%
Right at the Invoice Price - 14%
$75-$300 below invoice (17%)
$301-$400 below (6%)
$401-$600 below (9%)
$601-$1,000 below (16%)
<u>$1,001-$1,800 below (4%)</u>
Total Below Invoice - 52%
Total At or Below Invoice - 66%

• <u>**One of the best-selling compact crossover SUVs (190 reports)**</u>
$600-$1,500 over invoice (4%)
$400-$599 over (11%)
$200-$399 over (11%)
<u>$50-$199 over (11%)</u>
Total Over Invoice - 37%
Right at the Invoice Price - 11%
$50-$300 below invoice (15%)
$301-$500 below (15%)
$501-$800 below (11%)
$801-$1,000 below (7%)
<u>$1,001-$1,700 below (4%)</u>
Total Below Invoice - 52%
Total At or Below Invoice - 63%

- **One of the best-selling compact passenger cars (140 reports)**
  $700-$1,300 over invoice (6%)
  $50-$699 over (18%)
  Total Over Invoice - 24%
  Right at the Invoice Price - 10%
  $75-$200 below invoice (16%)
  $201-$400 below (12%)
  $401-$600 below (11%)
  $601-$1,000 below (17%)
  $1,001-$2,300 below (10%)
  Total Below Invoice - 66%
  Total At or Below Invoice - 76%

- **One of the best-selling minivans (168 reports)**
  $100-$600 over invoice (5%)
  Total Over Invoice - 5%
  Right at the Invoice Price - 5%
  $1-$500 below invoice (16%)
  $501-$800 below (25%)
  $801-$1,000 below (10%)
  $1,001-$1,200 below (16%)
  $1,201-$1,400 below (8%)
  $1,401-$1,700 below (10%)
  $1,701-$2,200 below (5%)
  Total Below Invoice - 90%
  Total At or Below Invoice - 95%

- **Another best-selling midsize passenger car (70 reports)**
  $100-$400 over invoice (6%)
  Total Over Invoice - 6%
  Right at the Invoice Price - 3%
  $1-$200 below invoice (11%)
  $201-$400 below (12%)
  $401-$700 below (18%)
  $701-$1,200 below (18%)
  $1,201-$1,400 below (18%)
  $1,401-$1,800 below (9%)

$1,801-$2,000 below (5%)
Total Below Invoice - 91%
Total At or Below Invoice - 94%

• **The best-selling series of an import luxury car (40 reports)**
$800-$1,500 over invoice (13%)
$500-$799 over (30%)
$100-$499 over (10%)
Total Over Invoice - 53%
Right at the Invoice Price - 15%
$200-$500 below invoice (10%)
$600-$1,300 below (15%)
$1,500-$1,900 below (7%)
Total Below Invoice - 32%
Total At or Below Invoice - 47%

Common sense query #1: If the invoice price were close to the real dealer cost, why would such a high percentage of these reports be below that number (with many way below)? Why were all those dealers willing to lose a lot of money on those sales?

• Our customers also report the dollar range of the competitive price proposals they receive — a range that's often wide enough to drive an 18-wheeler through. Here are a few examples, none of which include any customer or dealer cash incentives:

"Got my Acura TL for a whopping $1,535 below the dealer invoice. The other bids: $800 below, $550 over invoice, $1,000 over and $1,600 over. A $3,135 spread between the high and low bidder!"

F. B., Cordova, TN

"I paid $1,926 under invoice for a Ford SE Fusion Hybrid. The other seven bids were: $975 below invoice, $420 below, right at the invoice price, $150 over invoice, $200 over, $800 over and $1,500 over invoice. That was a difference of $3,426 from low to high."

S.V., Cedar Park, TX

"Our price for a Subaru Outback 2.5i Limited was $1,817 below the dealer invoice. Six other bids were: $1,817 below (tie with the winner), $445 below, $301 below, $191 below, $71 below, $196 over the invoice and $887 over. A $2,704 difference between the high and low bids."

S.P., Dowagiac, MI

"Purchased a Hyundai Tucson SE for $1,255 below invoice. These were the five other bids: $1,375 below (black only), $916 below, $472 below, $223 below and $1,019 over invoice. A $2,274 spread from top to bottom. I also qualified for $1,500 in rebates, which are not included in these numbers. I am a happy camper."

T.J., Stratford, CT

"The selling price on my Ford F-150 SuperCrew Lariat was $2,215 below the dealer invoice. The other bids were all under invoice. $1,254 below, $1,245 below, $1,200 below. $1,118 below, $1,100 below and $956 below. All bids shown are before subtracting $3,000 in rebates."

V.C., Dallas, TX

(To read other transaction reports, just visit our website — www.fightingchance.com — and click on the "Testimonials" button in the left column.)

Common sense query #2: If the invoice price were a dealer's real cost, why would there be such a wide difference between the high and low bids? And given that difference, wouldn't it be nuts for new-car shoppers to focus on a specific "target" or "Bottom Line Price," as Consumer Reports and those auto-pricing websites recommend?

Summarizing these real-world findings:

• A considerable number of new-car shoppers who really know their stuff are negotiating prices well below the dealer invoice price, before including any cash incentives. Yet none of the usual suspects that purvey their "expert" negotiating advice on the Internet are recommending target prices that get that low.

• When consumers know what they're doing and take control of the negotiation process, there's often an eye-popping difference between the high and low price proposals they get from dealers selling the same vehicle.

Don't these findings almost shout at us that "the invoice price" can't be close to the real price dealers end up paying for any vehicle? And that there must be other ways they get revenue to enable them to sell so many cars below that number?

Shouldn't this make you question whether any information source recommending target prices is giving you good advice?

In Chapter 7 ("I Heard It Through The Grapevine – 2nd Verse") we'll take another step in our search for the whole truth — a step based on more intelligence turned up by the 125,000 grapes on our vine.

But first, let's take a brief detour to let some of the hot air out of the "secret dealer cash" balloon that's been floated around for years by Consumer Reports and those other self-proclaimed experts.

"Time and the world do not stand still. Change is the law of life."

— John F. Kennedy

6 (Onion layer #4)

The way it is . . . . .
is not the way it was.

Once upon a time in the new-car business, there was an oft-used incentive called vehicle-specific "dealer cash." It was money almost all automakers paid dealers periodically for each unit of a given model they sold within a certain time period. (Henry Ford probably started the practice by telling his dealers in October 1908, "We'll give you fifty bucks for each Model T you sell by New Year's Eve. As long as it's black.")

The dealers could keep that cash as extra profit or pass some or all of it along to consumers, lowering the transaction price. Unlike factory-to-customer cash rebates, these dealer incentives were not advertised, and most new-car shoppers knew little or nothing about them.

Some car-buying websites imply that this incentive type is alive and well and widely used today. That's hogwash. It seems that they're still looking at the new-car business through their rear-view mirror, when they should be focused on the windshield to avoid exhibiting an embarrassing level of ignorance and crashing head-on into the truth.

Vehicle-specific factory-to-dealer cash incentives have been sliding toward extinction for years. A small number of brands still uses them, but typically only on vehicles that are: (1) well behind their sales objectives, (2) at the end of the model year, or (3) at the end of a model's multi-year design run.

To illustrate the fading role played today by these programs, I compiled a list of the May 2013 incentives reported for the Chicago market on auto websites I trust and combined it with the incentives shown in the bi-weekly national *CarDeals* report in the Fighting Chance information package. Here are the facts:

Of the 33 brands in the market, just 12 were offering vehicle-specific dealer cash – mostly in lieu of rebates.

• Acura, Infiniti, Volkswagen and Volvo, brands which accounted for just 5.4% of industry sales in 2012, had vehicle-specific dealer cash on all their models. Acura (Honda's upscale brand) never uses customer cash rebates, and Infiniti (Nissan's) almost never does. VW and Volvo performed relatively poorly in the first four months of 2013 and were angling for more volume. (The new-car market was up 6.9%, while VW sales were flat and Volvo was down 8.0%.).

• Mitsubishi, a brand down 6.5% in the first four months and hanging on by its fingernails in the U.S. market, placed vehicle-specific dealer cash on models accounting for 60% of its 2012 sales.

• Cadillac's dealer cash was on the CTS and the Escalade, which accounted for 47% of its 2012 sales, but were about to be replaced by redesigned 2014 versions. GM needed to move them out.

• The bulk of Chevy's vehicle-specific cash was on the critically important Malibu sedan, 11% of the brand's 2012 volume, but whose 2013 redesign was greeted by the sound of one hand clapping in the first four months: an 11.9% sales drop.

• Reeling from a 5.2% sales decline in the first four months, Mazda put dealer cash on 5 models accounting for 26% of its 2012 volume.

• Honda's dealer cash was on just two nameplates, built on the same platform and about to be "refreshed" or replaced by redesigned 2014 versions — the Odyssey and Pilot, 19% of the brand's 2012 sales.

• Lexus cash was only on IS models, which were 11% of brand sales in 2012, but tanked 22.3% in the first four months of 2013, as prospects were awaiting the arrival of the all-new 2014 model.

• GMC and BMW vehicle-specific cash offers were negligible, covering models representing just 5% and 3% of their 2012 volumes, respectively.

These other 21 brands had no such offers:

• Audi, Buick, Chrysler, Dodge, Fiat, Ford, Hyundai, Jaguar, Jeep, Kia, Land Rover, Lincoln, Mercedes-Benz, Mini, Nissan, Porsche, Ram, Scion, Smart, Subaru and Toyota. They almost never use this type of incentive. Together, they represented 63.2% of new vehicle sales in 2012.

Most telling, there was no vehicle-specific dealer cash on nameplates (models) that accounted for 89.3% of 2012 sales. I've been studying these kinds of numbers for over 20 years, and this is typical of the result you'd get most months in any major market. Few major-volume brands use vehicle-specific dealer cash, except sporadically and very selectively.

So if you're shopping for one of the more popular, better-selling models that's not near the end of its model year or about to be replaced by a redesign, you may be more likely to win the lottery than to find dealer cash attached to it.

Does that mean that automakers have eliminated dealer cash incentives?

No. They're spending more on them than ever before. But they're doing it differently, below everyone's radar. Over the last 18 years auto manufacturers have developed a myriad of truly-secret dealer incentive programs that are not attached to the sale of any specific vehicle. I estimate that over ninety percent of dealer cash dollars are allocated to these hidden bonus plans today.

The industry calls these "below-the-line" programs, invisible to consumers and consumer websites. They have several basic formats.

• They're frequently geared to overall sales targets that are set dealer-by-dealer. Big dealers get big targets; smaller dealers get smaller ones. But there's no way to learn any dealership's objective or where it stands vs. its target. You can't even learn when these programs begin and end. They can be monthly, bi-monthly, quarterly, whatever.

• If an incentive is focused on a specific vehicle, it's often based on stair-stepped sales targets. There are plateaus along the way, with dealers earning more money per car for all cars sold as they reach each higher sales level.

• Dealers can also get substantial bonus checks based on criteria other than sales results. For example, the cash reward may be tied to a dealer's sales total, but whether a dealership gets any bonus can depend on its success in meeting the automaker's standards in more subjective areas, such as Internet marketing and certified pre-owned sales programs, customer service, employee training, etc.

• Virtually all automakers tie bonuses to how well dealers treat their shared customers, based on how those people respond to post-purchase research questionnaires. Achieving the highest satisfaction scores on these "report cards" can earn dealerships big bucks, but sub-par ratings can cost them dearly.

• There's a myriad of variations of these basic formats, an array of which I've learned of from customers and describe in the next chapter. But those examples barely scratch the surface of all the hidden, "below-the-line" ways automakers can put money in dealers' pockets. These programs are limited only by the creative abilities of the car companies' marketing people.

I am convinced that all automakers use these kinds of hidden incentives, and that they are almost always present in some format, which effectively reduces the dealers' actual vehicle costs — often dramatically. This core fact leads me naturally to these conclusions:

• Given today's automaker/dealer financial relationship, it's bone-stupid to focus on any "target" or "ultimate underlying" price those "expert" auto websites give you.

• It's also nuts to take seriously advice that's based on an invoice price number that's a fiction we've all bought into, but a far cry from any dealer's real product cost.

• Dealer cash incentives may be hidden, but they can have a big impact on specific transaction prices, depending on where a given dealership stands vs. its targets at the time you're shopping for a new car. A car store getting close to a sales objective that will deliver a big (often six- or seven-figure) cash pile doesn't care how much it makes or loses on your deal.

• With different kinds of "below-the-line" cash programs almost always in effect, there's no dealership in the country that always makes the most aggressive price deals. The one making the best offer this month may be the high bidder a month or more later.

Additional fact: There is usually relatively little difference from one market to another in the average price paid for a given vehicle. Car buyers in Portland, ME are no smarter or dumber than those in Portland, OR. Ditto for the respective dealers. Assuming adequate sample sizes, I'd be shocked if the two U.S. markets with the highest and lowest average prices for a popular $25,000 car were much more than about $500 apart. (How far would you fly to save $500?)

But, as illustrated dramatically near the end of Chapter 5, there is almost always a significant difference between price proposals you'll get from dealers in the same market, depending on which ones are close to a pot of gold that you can't learn about. My customers typically report at least a $1,000 difference between the high and low price proposals on a popular $25,000 vehicle. And this time's low bidder may be next time's high bidder.

This argues for casting a relatively wide net, involving several dealerships in a competitive bidding process. If your objective is to get the best price available on the vehicle you want, you won't reach it if you restrict your search to just a few dealers.

In net, financial reality in the automobile business isn't anything like it was before the Internet arrived. And I'm convinced that anyone who isn't telling you that either doesn't know the truth or doesn't want you to know it.

Now let's take a gander at the wide range of specific "below-the-line" examples my customers have reported.

"I heard it through the grapevine" (2nd verse)

Smokey Robinson & The Miracles/1966
Gladys Knight & The Pips/1967
Marvin Gaye/1968
Creedence Clearwater Revival/1970
The California Raisins/1986
James Bragg & The Informants/1992-2013

7 (Onion layer #5)

"Loose lips sink ships."

This idiomatic wartime advice is worth remembering in your everyday discourse with others. Its long form is, "Don't talk carelessly. You never know who is going to hear what you say and how they will use what they hear."

Those 125,000 Fighting Chance customers aren't just smart shoppers, they're also really good listeners. When they're conversing with dealer employees, they are "all ears" (250,000 of them). Because frequently those employees get "loose lipped," sharing inside information they probably shouldn't, and our customers pass it along to us.

Hearing is believing. Especially when it comes from the retail horse's mouth.

This chapter illustrates the wide range of the revealing "below-the-line" insights our customer "spies" have heard at stores where they buy or lease. (Note that all of the prices reported in relation to the invoice are figured *before* subtracting any incentives in effect.)

• When an all-new design is introduced, we tell customers to wait two or three months to shop because the early demand usually exceeds the early supply, and dealers aren't dealing much off the sticker price. The deals get much better after the initial sales excitement dissipates. (It always does.) But a customer's wife wanted a totally redesigned popular midsize sedan in its first week on the market, and as he told me, "It's much cheaper to trade in cars than to trade in wives."

Nine of the ten price proposals he received via the competitive bidding process we recommend were at the full MSRP. But the tenth dealer sold him the car for $568 below the total dealer invoice price, about $2,500 less than any other store. In week #1!

The owner of the dealership took him aside quietly and said, "I want to tell you why I did that. My overall sales target for this period (surely at least 6 months) is 1,000 new cars. I'm at 964 now, and I'm doing whatever I have to do to get that bonus check, which I can almost taste." He didn't reveal the amount, but I guessed that the bonus at stake was at least $250 per vehicle and more likely $500 — a half million bucks.

I discussed this by phone several weeks later with someone I've known for over 25 years, one who had retired after managing a competitive brand's advertising and promotion programs for many years. His response was, "Your estimate is a tad low. When I was running programs like that, the payment was between $1,200 and $1,800 per vehicle." (You can do the math.)

• A customer got a "hot" redesigned compact SUV right at the dealer invoice during the introductory period, when most were selling at the full sticker price like Slurpees on a hot August day in Death Valley. The sales manager said, "You bought a great vehicle. The factory just released the 'recap money' on the last day of the month. It's $600 per car, and it only happens twice a year. I'm only sharing this information with you 'cause I could tell that you had done your homework up front."

• A woman who got her new Japanese midsize sedan for $800 below the invoice price reported, "The sales manager told me that my purchase and the others that day helped them hit the total target the factory had set for them, and the dealership would get $1,000 for every car sold during that period, the length of which he didn't identify."

• A customer who paid $1,315 below invoice for a compact Korean brand crossover was told this by a sales manager who *wasn't* the successful bidder: "A lot of dealers will hit their bonus. That means they will get $500 to $1,000 from the automaker for every car they sell. They must be close to that number. That's why their price was so low."

Shouldn't we ask Consumer Reports and those online new-car pricing "experts" we trust how they'd figure "the *real price* the dealer pays for the car" if he gets another hidden $250 or $500 or $1,200 or $1,800 for each one he sells? Especially when he knows those dollars were set aside to fund "below-the-line" programs that reduce his *real price* dramatically?

• A newly-redesigned Japanese compact sedan was almost impossible to deal on during its introductory period. But two customers in different cities got theirs then for $400 and $750 below the dealer invoice.

Both were told, "What we didn't earn on your deal was peanuts compared to the bonus we'll get for reaching our overall sales target."

• A driving enthusiast got his $70,000+ Special Edition European sports car, only 125 units of which were built for the U.S., for just $500 over invoice. "It was the end of the promotion period, and the dealership needed one more sale to meet its sales goal."

• Another customer got his Detroit-made half-ton pickup for $3,100 below invoice. The dealer told him he sold at that price because the sale got him to his bonus target.

• Here's one from my experience: We bought our daughter a compact SUV. A restyled, re-engineered model had arrived the previous month, and most bids were $800 to $1,300 over invoice. But the winning dealer's bid was $450 below invoice — $1,250 under the next best offer. As I signed the papers, I asked him why. His answer: "I didn't care if I lost money on your deal. I needed to sell three more cars to reach my target."

Obvious conclusion: Yes, there's hidden "dealer cash" on every car sold in one of these programs if a dealership reaches its total sales target for the period, but often none if it doesn't. And because every store's target is different, there's really no way to know where any dealership stands, or even when these incentive programs start and stop.

• A customer paid $2,317 below invoice for one of the most popular Japanese midsize sedans. The sales manager said he lost over $1,500 on the sale. Then he added, "I did that because the automaker has us on a 'stair-step' incentive program, with different levels. As we reach each higher target, we get more money per car for all the cars we've sold. Your sale got us to the next plateau."

• A customer shopping for a popular compact car of the same brand was told by the sales manager, "Your sale took me to the next level in the factory's bonus program."

• Another customer paid $958 below invoice for the same car. The winning dealer said that he'd met his target, and the automaker was giving him $750 for each car sold during the promotion period.

• When a couple paid $2,000 below invoice for Detroit's best-selling pickup in December, a friend at the dealership told them, "Your purchase got us to the annual sales level for that truck that earns us an extra $750 for every unit sold this year." For an average dealer selling 20 per month, that was $180,000. (Some dealers sell 30 or 40 each month.)

These programs can also be structured so that the dollars-per-car incentive is lower on less-expensive trim levels than on more-profitable higher trim levels.

The targets are often based on exceeding last year's sales in the same period. But during the worst months of the recession in 2009, when beating year-ago was a pipe dream, some customers shopping for different makes were told by salespeople that their dealerships could earn monthly bonuses by beating *last month's sales* (not last year's sales).

• A popular Korean SUV sold right at the invoice price. The dealer then deducted another $500, saying that the automaker gives him another $500 for every car he sells at invoice under the automaker's "Same As Invoice" program.

• Here's another program that can be the reason a dealer would sell a car for little or no visible profit, or even at a loss. It's called "turn-and-earn," where automakers base future dealer allocations of hot-selling cars on current sales results. It's "sell one today, and that guarantees we'll send another in the future. Don't, and we won't." Late in the month, if dealers haven't reached their turn-and-earn target on a hot car, they might offer bargain-basement prices just to guarantee their future supply.

Example: A redesigned Japanese luxury sedan was impossible to deal on in its introductory months, when demand was well ahead of supply and everyone was paying the full sticker price. But a customer got one right at the invoice price, over $3,000 below the MSRP. The reason reported: "The dealer said he hadn't sold enough that month to reach the 'turn-and-earn' total he needed to guarantee a future month's supply."

• Then there are the quick "Hit & Run" offers, where car companies will reduce prices to dealers in selected markets for periods as short as one day on specific models they want to move quickly to reach a certain near-term sales objective. As an example, here's an email message a customer received from a European luxury car dealer:

"The factory has announced a $1,000 one-day 'dealer demo' program on the car you want this Friday. When factories are close to hitting their sales objectives, they sometimes will give us extra money to classify a new car as a 'dealer demo.' The car has to be in dealer inventory to qualify, but if you don't mind buying a car that has lost one day of warranty coverage, you can buy that car as 'used' and save an extra $1,000."

• Dealerships will sometimes cut the price on a deal just to help one lagging salesperson reach his or her personal sales objective. As one shopper reported, "Even though the dealership had met its total sales target from the factory, my salesman needed the sale to make his bonus, so the sales manager helped him by cutting the price enough to win the bidding."

• Here's another way dealers get significant hidden cash from automakers that can impact their transaction prices:

A major U.S. brand was aggressively prodding its dealers to upgrade their facilities to improve the brand's image, as well as their own. Many dealers balked at the major expenditure. But the automaker was paying big-time incentive money to dealers who complied with the program: up to $100,000 to small stores and as much as $1.5 million to the biggest ones. The sales manager at one store told a customer that if his dealership hadn't upgraded, "It could have been at a competitive pricing disadvantage to dealerships which were receiving that bonus cash."

• This next one is very important, and virtually all car companies use it in some form. It's the CSI, or Customer Satisfaction Index. As noted earlier, it's how automakers gauge how their dealers are treating their customers-in-common.

The CSI is an outgrowth of the sorry reputation dealers had developed over decades of treating customers poorly. So the car companies created a customer-graded "dealer report card" as the basis for a program that offers significant financial rewards to dealerships that have cleaned up their acts, but includes substantial financial penalties for those that haven't. (When Chrysler CEO Lee Iacocca retired in 1992, he walked out the door saying, "It's a hell of a pass we've come to when we have to pay our dealers to be nice to their customers!")

New-car buyers and lessees typically get a post-purchase questionnaire asking them to rate the quality of their dealer experience in several areas. Automakers use this research to give dealerships a CSI score. Dealers scoring below certain threshold levels can be penalized financially. Some may get no bonus, regardless of their sales performance against targets. Others may get lower allocations of hot-selling vehicles. So you will find sales people on you like red ants on a spilled snow cone, urging you to give them nothing but the highest rating on every question.

As an example of the CSI's importance, here's what one customer reported to us after buying a European import sedan: "The salesperson prepped us on the follow-up survey to be sure we answered 'excellent' to everything. She told us that this was very important to enable dealerships to get the factory financial incentives and thus be able to give the customers the good deals they do."

Here are several additional relevant customer quotes:

• The sales manager said, "Be sure to say nice things about us on the survey the company will be sending you."

• Everyone at the dealership was very interested in the customer satisfaction survey. The sales manager, our salesman and the guy who handed us the keys said, "Excellent is what we hope we've earned. If not, before sending your response, please let us earn an excellent."

• As they handed us the keys, they reminded us to rate them as 'excellent' on everything because "*even a 'good' brings us down.*"

• A woman got a great deal on her popular import midsize sedan, but when she signed the papers in the finance manager's office, he pressured her to buy insurance and warranty products she didn't want. The experience was so distasteful that she gave the dealership a poor report card. A week later the angry sales manager called to complain. "We gave you a great price on that car! Why did you do that?" She told him. The obvious reason he called her, of course, was that her poor ratings had cost the dealership a lot of bonus cash.

• Some dealers may be anxious enough to retain a great CSI rating to give you an exceptional deal. A customer who paid well below invoice for a midsize sedan reported: "The dealer had the #1 CSI ranking in Northern California and wanted to keep it. They went $250 below the next best bid, asking in return that I give them 100% 'Excellent' scores on each survey question. He'd sell at almost any price to keep that #1 rating!"

• After negotiations were finished by one of our customers on a European luxury brand cabriolet, a loose-lipped sales manager urged him to give the dealership the highest ratings on every question in the follow-up questionnaire. He let it slip that dealers for that brand can earn bonuses ranging from 0.5% to 4% of the total MSRP on every car they sell if they score well on those "customer report cards!" (Note: 4% of a $50,000-stickered car is $2,000.)

Here's a report that will make you sit up straight and take notice:

• An old friend has a neighbor who's the sales manager of a luxury car store that sells 100 to 125 new cars per month. He wouldn't identify the brand because he didn't want to get in trouble with his buddy, who told him, "We care about the price we get for the car, but we care as much or more about the scores we get on the follow-up questionnaire. We make a big deal of that with our customers. We say, 'If there's anything we haven't done to get 10 on a scale of 1 to 10 on all 27 questions, tell us and we'll do it.' Free oil changes, whatever." He added that, "All our customers agree to do that. And every month they do, the dealership gets a check for over $100,000!" (That's over $1,200,000 per year.)

• Another illustration of the importance of a good CSI rating: A Detroit automaker ran an "Employee Price/You Pay What We Pay" consumer promotion. That was a great price, about 5% below the total dealer invoice. But at the end of a couple of calendar quarters some Fighting Chance customers bought vehicles for as much as $2,000 below that "Employee Price" *before* subtracting any rebate in effect. They had dealers competing aggressively, each trying to lose more money than the others to make those June and September sales.

A dealer salesperson told one of them why: "The factory is running quarterly promotions in which we can earn six-figure bonuses by reaching our assigned sales targets. So we didn't care how much we lost on your deal. But to get that money, we also need to have a great customer satisfaction rating. So please give us nothing but the highest scores on all the questions."

It's not only the sales departments that are focused on their CSI scores. The service departments have the same obsession. My daughter had dealership service work done on her 6-year old SUV. When she picked up her car, the Service Manager handed her a paper that read: "Thank you for your recent visit to our Service Department. In a few days you may be receiving a phone call or a survey via email. The automaker will ask you to rate your experience on a Yes or No scale. Here are some questions they will ask:

1. Did your Service Consultant update you regarding status?
2. Was your vehicle ready when promised?
3. Was your Service Consultant knowledgeable?
4. Was your pickup time reasonable?

The phone Survey Question will be: On a scale of 1 to 10 (10 being the highest), how would you rate your overall experience?

If after reviewing these questions you do not feel you can answer each with a YES, or rate your overall experience a 10, please let me know right away. This score is extremely important to me, your Service Consultant and your Technician."

In many cases the Service Department's CSI score can be part of a store's overall CSI rating.

• Here's something else I hear from customers that I doubt you'll learn on those "expert" websites. "The dealership gets another $500 if I finance through the automaker's finance company, and they passed it along to me to win my business."

As an ex-marketing manager for consumer goods companies, I'll bet the automakers' market research shows that customers who finance through their subsidiaries (Toyota Financial Services, Ford Motor Credit, etc.) are more likely to buy another of their vehicles in the future than those who don't. So they're happy to pay their dealers a cash bonus when they "walk the company finance line."

That's often the best choice for consumers, too. If you qualify for it (not everybody does), automaker financing frequently beats that from your bank or credit union. That's because car companies can take some of the profit they make selling cars to dealers and use it to "subvent" (reduce/buy down) the interest rate significantly.

There's usually no prepayment penalty if you pay off the loan relatively quickly, so why not ask if you'd get a better price if you financed that way, even if you plan to pay cash?

This is the kind of inside information we get regularly from our spies . . . . . . er, customers.

This 250,000-ear customer "grapevine" is not our sole source of "below-the-radar" information on how new-car dealers are secretly compensated. Your author does a little spying, too. My ears have been so close to the ground on this subject for so long, they're growing weeds.

Over the years, I've also talked periodically to smart people I've known who have been employed in or close to the new-car business. Everything I've learned from them lends credence to the conclusion that dealers get substantial hidden revenue from automakers — cash that dramatically reduces the net cost of their vehicles and boosts their profits.

I could add another 20 pages of specifics these friends have told me, but to avoid making this book longer than Tolstoy's *War and Peace*, I'll touch on just two of them.

• These hidden programs often have so many moving pieces that they defy description and make analysis a fool's errand. As an example, here's how a friend described an automaker's bonus plan one year:

- The automaker paid a bonus of 0.5% of the full retail/sticker price to dealers who delivered 75% of their monthly new-car sales target, increasing in stair steps to 1.25% to dealers who reached 125% of the target.

- Dealers who delivered 100% of both their new-car <u>and</u> used-vehicle sales targets <u>and</u> 40% of a separate factory-certified pre-owned vehicle sales target earned an additional 0.5% of sticker on all new-vehicle sales. That bonus bumped up to 1% of MSRP for hitting 60% of the certified pre-owned goal.

Got it? (I wish I did.)

Auto-info websites may occasionally advertise that their pricing reports include unpublished dealer incentives. How can they possibly do that when dealers are motivated by bonus plans like this? Wouldn't you love to be a fly on their office wall, watching them try to calculate the "unpublished" bonus dollar numbers for that company's dealers?

• There's also an important hidden element called "the dealer discount" that may boost dealer compensation further. Some of my customers have heard about this from folks in car stores after their deals were done. Apparently there's a basic, "visible" dealer discount (the difference between the invoice and retail prices that are available to consumers) and a more substantial "invisible" dealer discount that's hidden "below-the-line."

After hearing this, I contacted an old friend who's a total automobile junkie. He reads everything written about cars and the car business, frequently in public libraries that have publications he doesn't receive. He researched "dealer discounts" for me and came back with a specific example: an import luxury car brand for which that invisible "dealer discount" came close to doubling the gross profit percentage built into the new-car pricing that we all find on the Internet.

From 7% to 13.5%!

I can't tell you whether this element (a) includes some or all of the myriad types of "below-the-line" programs covered earlier in this chapter, or (b) is a separate, additional way dealers get compensated.

If any folks reading this chapter still doubt that the kinds of "below-the-line" dealer incentives it's covered account for the vast bulk of the money spent on "dealer cash" today, they should read this statement from a 1/16/14 *Wall Street Journal* article about new-car supplies getting higher and car sales slowing to single-digit yearly gains: *"That turns up pressure on auto dealers, ... as car makers tie payments to dealers to hitting certain sales quotas."*

Have you ever learned anything like you've read here on any of those auto-pricing websites?

If you still believe that the dealer invoice price minus "holdback" is anywhere near the "true cost" dealers pay for cars, it's time for you to wake up and smell the truth.

The most exciting phrase to hear, the one that heralds new discoveries, is not "Eureka, I've found it!," but "Gee, that's funny."

— Isaac Asimov
Science fiction novelist & scholar (1920 – 1992)

8 (Onion layer #7)

Hiding (in plain sight)

You've learned that "below-the-line" incentive programs are rampant throughout the industry. And that they can impact dramatically the 'real dealer cost' of every vehicle, and therefore the transaction prices a dealership is willing to offer to reach its secret sales targets.

To complete our search, we must answer the pivotal question these programs raise: *What's the missing link, the source of that substantial "below-the-line" money I hear about so frequently from my customers? Where is it hiding?*

Common sense says that since the bulk of a car company's revenue comes from its dealers, that money obviously must be hiding somewhere in the initial amount they pay for the vehicles — *the dealer invoice price.*

But how did that money get in there? An airtight case requires irrefutable evidence. A money trail to "connect the dots" from dealers to automakers and back to dealers.

The big breakthrough came early in 2011.

Sometimes the answer to the most puzzling question is right under your nose. When I stumbled and fell over this one, I asked myself, "Where have you been for the last 10 or 15 years, Bird Brain?"

First, a little backgound. One of the key elements in the Fighting Chance information package is a listing of current dealer invoice and retail/sticker pricing for every trim level of each vehicle. Automakers typically increase their prices throughout the model year. I get a download of new and revised pricing every week.

In January 2011, Toyota raised prices on eleven vehicles which accounted for 66% of its sales.

Examining this increase, I noticed that on eight vehicles Toyota had raised the base dealer invoice price by a lot more than it raised the base MSRP/sticker price. On three other vehicles the invoice price increased significantly, but the sticker price was unchanged.

Here are those numbers:
- Avalon: +$459-$493/invoice, +$150/sticker
- Camry: +$290-$384/invoice, +$100/sticker
- Venza: +$403-$434/invoice, +$150/sticker
- Yaris: +$224-$240/invoice, +$100/sticker
- 4Runner: +$461-$535/invoice, +$150-$180/sticker
- Highlander: +$411-$612/invoice, +$150-$200/sticker
- RAV4: +$443-$517/invoice, +$100/sticker
- Sequoia: +$806-$1009/invoice, +$450/sticker
- FJ Cruiser: +$253-$268/invoice, no increase/sticker
- Tacoma: +$164-$275/invoice, no increase/sticker
- Tundra: +$240-$424/invoice, no increase/sticker

After saying, "Gee, that's funny," I thought, "That makes no sense." Toyota had a terrible year in 2010, when charges of unintended acceleration damaged the brand's safety reputation and cut its U.S. sales by about 119,000 vehicles. That forced Toyota dealers to deal on price more aggressively that year than ever before to dig themselves out of the hole the company had dug for them.

There was no way Toyota would have rewarded their loyalty with price increases that cut their gross profit potential (markup on cost-of-goods to cover overhead and profit) by several hundred dollars on the bulk of the lineup. The dealers would have screamed like stuck pigs.

But they didn't.

And their silence spoke loudly.

It bred the strong suspicion that dealers supported these moves . . . and that the reason for this price change might be to build extra money into the invoice price that would flow back to dealers later without being detected by consumers or consumer websites.

Think again about "our retail store" selling flat-screen TVs. Remember how we'd have reacted if our real product costs were suddenly all over the Internet? How we'd demand that suppliers find a way to get money to us that no one could find out about?

Surely car dealers had reacted the same way when the Internet and those auto-pricing websites sucker-punched them in the 1990s.

I thought, "Maybe this Toyota scenario is an example of the factory-dealer financial arrangement that's been struck to address that problem."

Two more steps were needed to turn this speculation into certainty. I had to confirm that this Toyota move wasn't just a one-time pricing aberration, but a current example of a longer-term, ongoing practice. I also had to determine that Toyota wasn't a lone wolf . . . that the other brands had been on the same page of the industry's manual for that "redesign" of the automaker-dealer financial deal.

It's time to dig out the truth — *the whole truth* — that no one else is telling you.

A-ha moment:
*"A flash of insight that makes the
solution to a problem become clear."*

9 (Finally, the Onion's Core)

Eureka!

As noted in an earlier chapter, before the Internet enveloped the world in the mid-1990s, consumers could buy paperbacks listing dealer invoices for new cars and trucks. Some car shoppers did; most didn't. Those who did believed those listings were at least close to the real dealer costs, and they probably were then.

I thought if I could find a couple of those old books, I could examine the difference between the pre-Internet new-car pricing structures and 2011's, model by model.

My indispensable long-term assistant hit the "mother lode" when he found 1991 and 1993 pricing books on Amazon for 99 cents each (plus shipping). And those old paperbacks coughed up the hidden source of those hefty "below-the-line" dealer cash payments.

We compared the gross profit percentages built into the base sticker prices of the highest trim levels of several brands' models in 1991 and 1993, before the Internet mushroomed in 1995, with those in 2011 on comparable vehicles. (The base invoice and sticker prices account for the lion's share of their totals. And the most expensive models typically carry the highest gross profit percentages.)

We started with Toyota, and what we found in that pricing information wasn't just eye-opening, it was a bombshell!

Our "A-ha moment" arrived when we saw that the gross profit percentages in Toyota's retail prices had dropped dramatically over that 18- to 20-year period. And all our "Gee, that's funny" statements quickly changed to "So that's how they did it!"

Check out the following changes in Toyota's gross profit (markup on cost-of-goods-sold) percentage numbers between the early 1990s and 2011. (Note that some model names have changed over the years for vehicles that have occupied the same size-and-price niche in the brand's lineup.)

- **Camry: 1993** – 16.0% **2011** – 9.0%
- **Corolla: 1993** – 14.0% **2011**– 7.3%
- **Tercel: 1993** – 14.0% **Yaris: 2011** – 4.0%
- **4Runner: 1993** – 15.5% **2011** – 8.0%
- **Land Cruiser: 1991** – 16.5% **2011** – 10.5%
- **Larger Pickup: 1991** – 15.5% **Tundra: 2011** – 7.5%
- **Compact Pickup: 1991** – 14.0% **Tacoma: 2011** – 7.3%

When we took that same walk down Memory Lane with other brands, we found the same pattern. It was an industry-wide phenomenon!

Gross Profit % In The Base Sticker Price

Audi
- **1993** 90 Sedan – 15.2% **2011** A4 Sedan – 7.0%
- **1993** 100 Wagon – 16.4% **2011** A4 Avant – 7.0%

BMW
- **1993** 3-Series Rag Top – 16.3% **2011** 3-Series Rag Top – 8.0%
- **1993** 5-Series Sedan – 16.2% **2011** 5-Series Sedan – 8.0%
- **1993** 7-Series Sedan – 18.2% **2011** 7-Series Sedan – 8.0%

Buick
- **1993** Le Sabre – 12.5% **2011** Lucerne – 4.0%
- **1993** Century – 12.5% **2011** LaCrosse – 4.0%
- **1993** Regal – 12.5% **2011** Regal – 4.0%

Cadillac
- **1993** DeVille – 13.5% **2011** DTS – 5.5%
- **1993** Seville – 13.5% **2011** STS – 5.5%

Chevrolet Cars
- **1993** Corsica – 9.5% **2011** Malibu – 5.0%
- **1993** Camaro – 8.5% **2011** Camaro – 4.0%
- **1993** Cavalier – 9.5% **2011** Cruze – 4.0%
- **1993** Corvette – 14.5% **2011** Corvette – 6.5%
- **1993** Lumina – 12.5% **2011** Impala – 4.0%

Chevrolet Trucks
- **1993** S-10 Blazer – 9.5% **2011** Equinox – 5.0%
- **1991** Silverado 1500 – 13.7% **2011** Silverado 1500 – 7.0%
- **1991** Silverado 2500 – 13.7% **2011** Silverado 2500 – 7.0%
- **1991** Silverado 3500 – 13.7% **2011** Silverado 3500 – 7.0%
- **1991** Suburban – 13.7% **2011** Suburban – 7.0%
- **1991** Full-Size Blazer – 13.7% **2011** Tahoe – 7.0%

Chrysler
- **1993** Concorde – 12.7% **2011** 300 – 5.0%
- **1993** LeBaron – 10.8% **2011** 200 – 4.3%
- **1993** Town & Country – 10.4% **2011** Town & Country – 6.0%

Dodge
- **1993** Daytona – 9.5% **2011** Avenger – 4.2%
- **1993** Intrepid – 12.9% **2011** Charger – 4.5%
- **1993** Grand Caravan – 9.9% **2011** Grand Caravan – 5.4%
- **1991** Ram 1500 – 13.6% **2011** Ram 1500 – 7.5%
- **1991** Ram 2500 – 13.9% **2011** Ram 2500 – 8.3%
- **1991** Ram Charger – 13.7% **2011** Durango – 6.1%

Ford
- **1993** Escort – 10.3% **2011** Focus – 6.9%
- **1993** Mustang – 10.4% **2011** Mustang – 8.1%
- **1993** Taurus – 14.3% **2011** Taurus – 8.2%
- **1993** Explorer – 11.4% **2011** Explorer – 7.0%
- **1991** Bronco – 13.9% **2011** Expedition - 7.1%

GMC
- **1993** Jimmy – 9.5% **2011** Terrain – 5.0%
- **1991** Sierra 1500 – 13.7% **2011** Sierra 1500 – 7.0%
- **1991** Sierra 2500 – 13.7% **2011** Sierra 2500 – 7.0%
- **1991** Sierra 3500 – 13.7% **2011** Sierra 3500 – 7.0%
- **1991** Full-Size Jimmy – 13.7% **2011** Yukon – 7.0%
- **1991** Suburban – 13.7% **2011** Yukon XL – 7.0%

Honda
- **1993** Accord Sedan – 16.0% **2011** Accord Sedan – 9.4%
- **1993** Civic Sedan – 15.0% **2011** Civic Sedan – 8.0%

Hyundai
- **1993** Elantra Sedan – 11.7% **2011** Elantra Sedan – 4.2%
- **1993** Excel – 9.8% **2011** Accent – 2.9%
- **1993** Sonata – 12.3% **2011** Sonata – 6.5%

Infiniti
- **1993** G20 Sedan – 20.0% **2011** G37 Sedan – 7.7%

Jeep
- **1993** Cherokee – 9.9% **2011** Liberty – 3.4%
- **1993** Grand Cherokee – 9.9% **2011** Grand Cherokee – 6.0%
- **1993** Wrangler 2-door – 9.1% **2011** Wrangler 2-door – 5.9%

Land Rover
- **1991** Range Rover – 17.9% **2011** Range Rover – 9.0%

Lincoln
- **1993** Town Car – 15.3% **2011** Town Car – 6.2%

Lexus
- **1994** ES Sedan – 18.0% **2011** ES Sedan – 9.3%
- **1994** GS Sedan – 18.0% **2011** GS Sedan – 11.0%
- **1994** LS Sedan – 20.0% **2011** LS Sedan – 11.0%

Mazda
- **1993** Protégé – 9.9% **2011** Mazda3 – 6.4%
- **1993** Mazda 626 – 12.9% **2011** Mazda6 – 7.6%
- **1993** Miata – 10.9% **2011** Miata MX-5 – 7.5%
- **1993** RX-7 – 15.0% **2011** RX-8 – 7.4%
- **1993** MPV – 10.9% **2011** Mazda5 – 6.4%

Mercedes-Benz
- **1993** 190E – 17.0% **2011** C-Class – 7.0%
- **1993** 300-Class – 17.0% **2011** E-Class – 7.0%
- **1993** S-Class – 17.0% **2011** S-Class – 7.0%

Mitsubishi
- **1993** Mirage – 12.0% **2011** Lancer – 4.2%
- **1993** Eclipse Coupe – 13.0% **2011** Eclipse Coupe – 5.4%
- **1993** Galant – 15.0% **2011** Galant – 4.2%

Nissan
- **1993** Sentra – 11.8% **2011** Sentra – 6.8%
- **1993** Altima – 13.3% **2011** Altima – 7.3%.
- **1993** Maxima – 13.3% **2011** Maxima – 8.4%
- **1991** 4WD Pickup – 11.3% **2011** 4WD Frontier – 7.3%

Subaru
- **1993** Legacy Sedan – 12.1% **2011** Legacy Sedan – 6.8%
- **1993** Legacy Wagon – 12.1% **2011** Outback – 6.4%

Volkswagen
- **1993** Fox Sedan – 9.1% **2011** Jetta Sedan – 4.0%
- **1993** Passat – 11.8% **2012** Passat – 4.1% (there was no 2011)

Volvo
- **1993** 240 Sedan – 10.4% **2011** S80 Sedan – 6.0%
- **1993** 240 Wagon – 10.6% **2011** XC70 – 6.0%

But was this a recent phenomenon, or had it been going on unnoticed for years?

Going back to Amazon, we found eleven similar books that were published through 2004. (We had all the 2005 and subsequent-year pricing in our files.) Analyzing them, we discovered that the gross profit percentage built into the sticker price had been reduced dramatically over a period of several years in a gradual, multi-step process that differed from automaker to automaker and vehicle to vehicle. That prevented consumers from noticing a sudden dramatic change that would raise questions about the relationship of the dealer invoice price to a real "dealer cost" number.

Using one or more vehicles of each brand for illustration, the following time-line progression shows that those step-by-step changes continued through the 2013 model year. You can bet it's still an active process. (I'm listing the vehicles by their current names, not those of their same-size predecessors shown in the previous table. For vehicles that were not sold in the early 1990s, I've shown the reduction in the base gross profit percentage from the earliest year available.)

- **Acura MDX: 2002** – 10.0% **2007** – 9.4% **2008** – 9.1% **2011** – 8.4% **2013** – 7.6%.
- **Acura TL Sedan: 1994** – 15.2% **1996** – 13.2% **1998** – 10.7% **2000** – 9.8% **2003** – 8.8% **2007** – 8.3% **2008** – 8.1% **2011** – 7.2% **2013** – 6.4%
- **Acura TSX Sedan: 1994** – 14.1% **1996** – 12.1% **1998** – 10.7% **2000** – 9.8% **2004** – 8.8% **2007** – 8.2% **2008** – 8.0% **2011** – 7.0% **2013** – 6.2%
- **Audi A4 Sedan: 1993** – 15.2% **1995** – 12.1% **2000** – 11.1% **2002** – 9.1% **2007** – 7.4% **2011-2013** – 7.0%
- **Audi Allroad: 1993** – 16.4% **1998** – 11.5% **2000** – 10.6% **2002** – 9.2% **2007** – 7.4% **2011-2013** – 7.0%
- **BMW 3-Series Convertible: 1993** – 16.3% **1995** – 15.9% **1996** – 13.6% **1998** – 12.4% **2000** – 9.5% **2002** – 8.6% **2011-2013** – 8.0%
- **BMW 5-Series Sedan: 1993** – 16.2% **1998** – 12.4% **2000** – 9.7% **2002** – 8.7% **2011-2013** – 8.0%
- **BMW 7-Series Sedan: 1993** – 18.2% **1996** – 13.9% **1998** – 12.5% **2000** – 9.8% **2002** – 8.7% **2011-2013** – 8.0%

- **Buick LaCrosse:** **1993** – 12.5% **1995** – 10.5% **2000** – 8.5% **2007** – 5.5% **2011-2013** – 4.0%
- **Buick Regal:** **1993** – 12.5% **1996** – 8.5% **2011** –**2013** - 4.0%
- **Chevrolet Malibu:** **1993** – 9.5% **1998** – 8.5% **2007-2013** – 5.5%
- **Chevrolet Corvette:** **1993** – 14.5% **1998** – 12.5% **2007** – 10.5% **2011-2013** – 6.5%
- **Chevrolet Impala:** **1993** – 12.5% **1995** – 9.5% **1998** – 8.5% **2007-2013** – 5.5%
- **Chevrolet Cruze:** **1993** – 9.5% **1995** – 7.5% **1998** – 6.5% **2007** – 5.5% **2011-2013** – 4.0%
- **Chrysler 300:** **1993** – 12.7% **1995** – 10.0% **2000** – 8.8% **2003** – 8.3% **2005** – 7.4% **2007** – 7.0% **2011** – 5.0% **2013** – 3.4%
- **Chrysler 200:** **1993** – 10.8% **1994** – 10.3% **2000** – 8.7% **2003** – 7.7% **2011-2013** – 4.5%
- **Chrysler Town & Country:** **1993** – 10.4% **1994** – 9.6% **2002** – 8.9% **2011** – 6.0% **2012** – 5.0% **2013** – 4.6%
- **Dodge Charger:** **1993** – 12.9% **1995** – 10.1% **1998** – 8.7% **2004** – 7.5% **2007** – 6.9% **2011** – 4.5% **2012-2013** – 3.6%
- **Dodge Grand Caravan:** **1994** – 10.0% **2002** – 9.0% **2005** – 8.5% **2011** – 5.4% **2013** – 4.8%
- **Ford Explorer:** **1993** – 11.4% **1996** – 10.3% **2003** – 9.6% **2008** – 7.2% **2011** – 7.0% **2013** – 6.8%
- **Ford Mustang:** **1993** – 10.4% **1995** – 10.0% **1996** – 9.1% **2002** – 8.5% **2011** – 8.1% **2013** – 7.7%
- **Honda Accord:** **1993** – 16.0% **1995** – 11.6% **2000** – 11.1% **2002** – 10.0% **2011** – 9.4% **2012-2013** – 8.5%
- **Honda Civic:** **1993** – 15.0% **1995** – 10.3% **2000** – 9.7% **2002** – 8.6% **2011** – 8.0% **2012-2013** – 7.1%
- **Honda Odyssey:** **1996** – 11.6% **2000** – 11.1% **2002** – 10.0%. **2011** – 9.4% **2012-2013** – 8.6%
- **Honda CR-V:** **1997** – 9.3% **2000** – 8.7% **2002** – 7.8% **2003** – 7.6% **2011** – 7.0% **2012-2013** – 6.1%
- **Hyundai Accent:** **1993** – 9.8% **1998** – 7.4% **2000** – 6.4% **2011-2013** – 2.9%.
- **Hyundai Elantra:** **1993** – 11.7% **1998** – 10.4% **2000** – 8.0% **2007** – 7.5% **2011-2013** – 4.2%
- **Hyundai Sonata:** **1993** – 12.3% **1998** – 11.9% **2000** – 10.8% **2002** – 9.8% **2011-2013** – 6.5%

- **Infiniti G Sedan: 1993** – 20.0% **1995** – 16.0% **1996** – 15.2% **2003** – 9.4% **2007** – 8.0% **2011** – 7.7% **2012-2013** – 7.4%
- **Jaguar XJ Sedan: 1995** – 18.4% **1996** – 15.9% **1998** – 12.6% **2007** – 8.9% **2011-2013** – 8.0%
- **Jeep Grand Cherokee: 1993** – 9.9% **2002** – 8.8% **2011** – 6.0% **2012-2013** – 5.0%
- **Jeep Wrangler 2-door: 1993** – 9.1% **2007** – 8.8% **2011** – 5.9% **2012-2013** – 5.8%
- **Kia Sportage: 1998** – 10.7% **2002** – 10.0% **2011-2013** – 6.7%
- **Kia Optima: 2002** – 11.6% **2003** – 8.9% **2007** – 7.4% **2011-2013** – 6.6%
- **Lexus ES Sedan: 1994** – 18.0% **1995** – 17.0% **1996** – 15.0% **1998** – 13.1% **2002** – 11.3% **2008** – 10.3% **2011** – 9.3%. **2012-2013** – 6.3%
- **Lexus GS Sedan: 1994** –18.0% **1995** – 17.0% **1996** – 15.0% **1998** – 14.1% **2007** – 13.0% **2008** – 12.0% **2011** – 11.0% **2013** – 7.0%
- **Lexus LS Sedan: 1994** – 20.0% **1995** – 18.0% **1996** -- 16.0% **1998** – 15.2% **2002** – 13.0% **2008** – 12.0% **2011** – 11.0% **2012-2013** – 8.0%
- **Lexus RX SUV: 2000** – 13.1% **2002** – 12.0% **2004** – 11.5% **2011** – 9.5% **2012-2013** – 6.5%
- **Lincoln Town Car: 1993** – 15.3% **1995** – 13.0% **1996** – 12.0% **1998** – 9.0% **2003** – 8.6% **2011** – 6.2%
- **Mazda3 Sedan: 1993** – 9.9% **1995** – 8.9% **2000** – 7.5% **2011** – 6.4% **2012-2013** – 4.4%
- **Mazda6 Sedan: 1993** – 12.9% **1995** – 10.9% **1998** – 10.0% **2000** – 8.8% **2002** – 7.8% **2011** – 7.6% **2013** – 5.6%
- **Mercedes C-Class Sedan: 1993** – 17.0% **1995** – 15.0% **1998** – 13.0% **2000-2013** – 7.0%.
- **Mercedes E-Class Sedan: 1993** – 17.0% **1996** – 13.0% **2000-2013** – 7.0%.
- **Mercedes S-Class Sedan: 1993** – 17.0% **1996** – 13.0% **2000-2013** – 7.0%
- **Mitsubishi Lancer: 1993** – 12.0% **1995** – 10.0% **2000** – 8.0% **2002** – 6.2% **2007** – 4.7% **2011-2013** – 4.2%
- **Nissan Sentra: 1993** – 11.8% **1995** – 10.8% **1996** – 9.4% **2000** – 8.6% **2011-2013** – 6.7%
- **Nissan Altima: 1993** – 13.3% **1995** – 12.4% **1998** – 10.0% **2000** – 9.1% **2004** – 7.5% **2011-12** – 7.3% **2013** – 8.6%

- **Nissan Maxima: 1993** – 13.3% **1995** – 12.5% **1996** – 11.0% **2000** – 10.1% **2004** – 8.6% **2011– 2013** – 8.4%
- **Nissan Pathfinder: 1993** – 12.3% **1996** – 10.0% **2002** – 9.1% **2003** – 8.9% **2011-2012** – 7.4% **2013** – 8.9%
- **Subaru Legacy Sedan: 1993** – 12.1% **1995** – 10.5% **2000** – 9.4% **2007** – 7.2% **2011-2012** – 6.8% **2013** – 6.2%
- **Subaru Outback Wagon: 1993** – 12.1% **1995** – 10.5% **2000** – 9.4% **2007** – 7.2% **2011-2013** – 6.4%
- **Subaru Forester: 1998** – 10.2% **2001** – 9.3% **2004** – 8.9% **2011-2013** – 6.4%
- **Toyota Camry: 1993** – 16.0% **1995** – 13.3% **1998** – 12.5% **2002** – 11.0% **2008** – 10.8% **2011-2013** – 9.0%
- **Toyota Corolla: 1993** – 14.0% **1995** – 12.3% **1998** – 11.4% **2003** – 9.5% **2011-2013** – 7.3%
- **Toyota 4Runner: 1993** – 15.5% **1996** – 13.2% **1998** – 12.5% **2003** – 10.7% **2008** – 9.7% **2011-2013** – 8.0%
- **Toyota RAV4: 1996** – 11.2% **1998** – 10.4% **2002** – 9.0% **2011-2013** – 6.5%
- **Toyota Sienna: 1996** – 13.3% **2000** – 12.4% **2002** – 11.0% **2011-2013** – 8.0%
- **VW Jetta Sedan: 1994** – 9.6% **1995** – 7.7% **2000** – 9.0% **2002** – 8.8% **2007** – 6.6% **2008** – 5.4% **2011-2013** – 4.0%
- **VW Passat: 1993** – 11.8% **1995** – 10.0% **2000** – 8.1% **2007** – 7.3% **2008** – 6.4%. **2011-2013** – 4.1%
- **Volvo S80 Sedan: 1994** – 14.0% **1995** – 9.5% **1996** – 8.6% **1998** – 8.4% **2000** – 8.2% **2002- 2013** – 6.0%
- **Volvo XC70: 1994** – 13.6% **1995** – 9.1% **1996** – 8.3% **1998** – 7.4% **2002-2013** – 6.0%

THE JAW-DROPPING CONCLUSION

Since the arrival of the Internet, automakers have removed 40% to 73% of the *visible* gross profit margin built into the sticker price and made it *invisible* by hiding it in the invoice price dealers pay initially, where it can be funneled back to dealers in "below-the-line" cash incentive and bonus programs that are invisible to consumers and consumer websites.

Clearly, a key objective of the pricing "redesign" program was to keep consumers believing what they'd believed for years: that the invoice price is "a legitimate dealer cost figure." That made it the ideal place to stash hidden dealer incentive dollars. The industry inflated the size of the invoice price gradually, year by year, to avoid easy detection. (This isn't rocket science. It's paper airplane science.)

This remains an ongoing process, with no end in sight. Note in the numbers above that the following brands have cut those percentages further since the 2011 model year: Acura, Chrysler, Dodge, Ford, Honda, Infiniti, Jeep, Mazda and Subaru.

Then there's Lexus, which became the "poster child" for this phenomenon with these price changes in the first quarter of 2012:

• The ES sedan accounts for about 25% of Lexus sales. The base gross profit was slashed from 9.3% on the 2011 model to 6.3% on the 2012. The sticker price was unchanged, leading consumers to think there'd been no price increase, but the invoice price was inflated by $1,101.

• The RX 350 SUV accounts for about 38% of sales. The base gross profit plunged from 9.5% on the 2011 to 6.5% on the 2012. The sticker price didn't move an inch, but the invoice price mushroomed by $1,214.

"Adjustments" were also made to the pricing of other Lexus models at the same time.

But wait, there's more! Lexus also discontinued its "holdback" then — 2% of the base sticker price, which consumers previously could learn was in the invoice price, then returned to dealers after a sale was made. That money is still there, but it's no longer "holdback" that dealers get automatically. Instead, it's allocated to other "below-the-line" incentive programs that no one can identify.

So in one slick stroke, Lexus took 5% of the base sticker price, previously visible to the consumer as potential gross profit dollars, and buried it in a number that most new-car shoppers perceive as "dealer cost" dollars. That "facade" effectively hid additional gross profits of $1,835 for the ES 350 and $2,024 for the RX 350, with absolutely no increase in the sticker price!

One result of this action: It enables Lexus dealers to thrill buyers with below-invoice deals today that aren't nearly as good as the same below-invoice deals would have been on 2011 models.

I'm not picking on Lexus. This is just a vivid illustration of the invoice-sticker "redesign" program all automakers began over 18 years ago to protect their dealers' profitability and have continued ever since.

As a result, the invoice price has become a bloated imposter for every auto brand.

It may be frustrating to you to learn this morsel of truth, but it is what it is. And it carries significant implications for consumers.

• <u>Fact</u>: These truly-secret programs are used industry-wide. They'd have to be.

Many dealership groups have several different brand franchises. It's like owning a mutual fund holding the common stocks of several corporations. The sun doesn't shine on the same dog every day, in either the stock market or the retail auto business, so it's smart not to put all your eggs in one automaker's basket.

Some of these groups are large, public companies, while others are privately held. In 2012 the 125 largest retailer groups owned over 2,600 dealerships. That's about 20 each, but a few have over 100.

A key objective for all automakers is to keep their "dealer principals" (the individuals, families or senior executives of the corporations which own the stores) more focused on their brand's business than on that of the other brands they represent.

That won't happen if their profit enhancement programs aren't competitive. So you can be sure the factories are all playing the "cash below-the-line" game aggressively.

EVERY NEW-CAR BUYER NEEDS
TO UNDERSTAND THESE CORE FACTS

1. The financial relationship between the automakers and their dealers has been completely and permanently changed. But not a single auto information source is telling you this game-changing fact.

2. The industry reacted to the negative impact of the easy availability of dealer invoice prices when the Internet arrived by launching a continuing program to systematically transfer beaucoup bucks from the sticker price to the invoice price — bucks that make "holdback" look like bus fare —disguising them there as dealer-cost dollars. (Remember, we're all babes in the woods, believing what we've been told.)

3. That realignment of the invoice-retail price relationship has drastically cut the "visible" gross profit in the MSRP by 40% to 73%. Today there's not a single new vehicle with more than a 10% difference between the invoice price — which dealers do pay initially — and the sticker price — which almost no consumer pays. The industry average is 6% to 8%. (It's just 7% for Mercedes, 4% to 5% for Volkswagen.) If the invoice were anything close to a true cost number, we'd return to

the horse-and-buggy era because there wouldn't be a single car store standing.

4. Those transferred dollars have fueled a dramatic increase in the money allocated to hidden, "below-the-line" dealer incentive programs. Today about 90% of the available dealer incentive dollars are not attached to the purchase of any specific vehicles. Many are based on overall sales targets that are set dealer-by-dealer. Others are geared to more subjective targets, like a dealership's customer satisfaction score. And there is no source that can disclose to you the details of the vast number and endless variety of "unpublished" dealer incentives.

5. With so much hidden incentive cash in those "below-the-line" programs, dealers will often sell some vehicles at prices way below their real cost if those sales help get them to a bonus target that will maximize their store's total profit.

6. As a result, there is no "right price to pay" for any car because no one can learn any dealer's "real cost." Not Kelley Blue Book. Not Edmunds. Not Cars.com. Not TrueCar. Not Consumer Reports. Not anyone. The "dealer invoice price minus holdback" used as a touchstone is typically not even a close approximation.

For example: In December 2013 a popular auto brand with over 1,000 dealers offered them a $3,000 bonus for each vehicle sold above those sold the previous December. Could any auto-information service tell us whether *any* dealers reached and exceeded that bonus sales level? (No.) And if so, which ones? (No.) My guess: many dealerships did, but more didn't. The brand's December sales ended just 2.4% above year-ago.

7. The *real price* dealers end up paying for vehicles is invisible to everyone except the owners of each dealership. That "true cost" number will differ from dealer to dealer. And for any given dealer, it will change from one "below-the-line" promotion period to the next. The dealer with the lowest price today may be the one with the highest price tomorrow, whether "tomorrow" is the next month, the next quarter, or the next year. That makes walking into a car store to negotiate or contacting only a few dealers a really bad idea.

8. In this new real world, using any recommended "target price" or making an offer is a bonehead play if your objective is to get the best price available in your market.

In summary, the "conventional wisdom" about how to buy or lease a new car that floods the Internet is based on the long-outdated assumption that the automaker-dealer financial world is essentially unchanged from its pre-Internet status. That world was flat, static, two-dimensional, open, uncomplicated, and easy to understand and describe accurately to consumers. It was one where you could "start with this number, add these numbers and subtract those, and *voila*, there it was — *the truth!*"

You don't need to be a Mensa member to examine "The Exhibit" that starts on page 72 and conclude that that flat world has been dead for well over a decade. Today the automaker-dealer financial world is round, dynamic, multi-dimensional, closed, complicated, and impossible to decipher to determine dollar values for any dealer's *true cost.* There are no numbers you can 'start with, add this and subtract that' and end up with anything but *"boomfog!"* (Boomfog — a word coined by an old friend: A meaningless statement or conclusion, unrelated to reality.)

In the next chapter we'll look at what I'm convinced is the real reason those online auto-pricing sources aren't telling you the truth — the whole truth — about new-car pricing.

"No man can serve two masters."

— Matthew 6:24

10

$ilence is golden.

There are several "corporate" new-car websites that car-shopping con-sumers turn to for information and advice.

I call them "corporate" because they are. Corporations of substantial size, most of them in business to earn profits for their creators and in-vestors. One, Consumer Reports, is a highly respected non-profit organ-ization. They're all shining examples of the American entrepreneurial spirit, each attracting millions of website visitors a month. In many ways I admire them. They're all run by smart cookies.

• They identified a need that signaled a big revenue opportunity: Consumers' desire to avoid getting taken in a purchase process where they feel mismatched, uninformed and financially vulnerable.

• And they created products to fill that need: Websites full of infor-mation we car shoppers think we should have, positioning themselves as consumer-oriented auto industry experts, recommending the target prices we should aim for and funneling us to dealers who will sell at those prices.

FOR-PROFIT SITES

Anyone who has spent time on these websites has surely noticed one or more of their intrusive elements, like a plethora of automaker advertising and a repetitive, two-lapel sales pitch urging you to "click through" to get dealer price proposals.

Their major revenue sources are: (1) advertising dollars from car companies and dealers, who pay them handsomely to reach millions of eyeballs; (2) small referral fees from their "network" dealers when visi-tors "click through" for price quotes; and (3) richer "finder's fees" from those dealers when those referrals turn into sales. (A common number: about $300, which, of course, is built into the price consumers pay.)

In states that prohibit dealers from paying third parties for sending them sales, dealers pay a "subscription" fee. Larger dealerships pay higher fees than smaller ones. Dealers consider those extra costs as they determine their price proposals to consumers.

Many of those for-profit sites provide valuable information for new-vehicle shoppers. Specs on the cars they're considering. Reviews of their pluses and minuses. Cost of ownership estimates between competing vehicles. And more. I use them often for that stuff.

But they get virtually all their revenue from the automobile business and none from you, the target audience they appear to serve. (We call them "consumer information sites," right?) Better stated, you're the target for the audience they truly serve, the automakers and dealers that provide their revenue.

Those sites are "third-party lead generators." They act as conduits for conveying shoppers to dealers, who turn them into buyers. Their paychecks are based on their ability to do that, and they do it very well. They're not doing anything illegal or immoral. They're not promising to get you the best price available in your market. They're sending you to dealers who will give you a "fair price," based importantly on "what others are paying," and an easy, no-hassle deal. And that's a valuable public service for consumers who'd rather have all their molars pulled than negotiate the price of a new car.

Understand, however, that visitors who "click through" for price bids are directed only to dealers in that site's "network." That can be a relatively small number of stores in your market. Dealers typically pay for leads from their market areas, and they don't cotton to competing with other nearby, same-brand dealers.

There may be "non-network" dealers for a brand in the same area that would sell for significantly less. But that site's visitors won't get bids from them. And often a more remote dealer will see you as a prospect he'd seldom attract and offer you a much better price than you'd get in your hometown.

Some sites may list the number of dealers in their national network by brand. To help you calculate a network's percentage of a brand's total dealer lineup, here's the number of U.S. stores each brand had on January 1, 2014:

Acura/275	Honda/1,042	Mercedes/361
Audi/280	Hyundai/825	Mitsubishi/386
BMW/338	Infiniti/205	Mini/119
Buick/2,081	Jaguar/163	Nissan/1,061
Cadillac/933	Jeep/2,275	Porsche/189

Chevrolet/3,035	Kia/770	Scion/1,003
Chrysler/2,300	Land Rover/167	Subaru/621
Dodge/2,302	Lexus/234	Toyota/1,234
Ford/3,118	Lincoln/917	VW/640
GMC/1,748	Mazda/636	Volvo/305

For example, you might get price proposals from only three dealers. After 20+ years teaching consumers how to conduct a truly productive competitive bidding process, I can assure you that contacting only three dealers doesn't cut it. That's like waving the white flag of surrender. In my view, that's not a negotiation, it's a capitulation.

If you simply want to buy a car for the dealer-friendly target prices close to those that other shoppers have actually paid, one, two or three dealers is enough to accomplish that modest goal. Those sites' network dealers will be delighted to get your business.

But if your objective is to get the best price available, you need at least six to ten dealerships agreeing to participate in a bona fide competitive bidding process.

Why? To have a better shot at contacting a store nearing a sales target that'll net it a big "below-the-line" bonus check and net you a big price break. And that will rarely happen if you choose to rely on any auto information site's limited dealer network.

CONSUMER REPORTS

Consumer Reports is our most respected and revered consumer organization. It's the one source we trust to give us pearls of truth and wisdom about the products and services we buy.

I'm a fan. My family doesn't make any significant purchase without checking its ratings.

Every major profit and nonprofit organization has a core set of values and behaviors that guide its actions, starting with a mission statement about its *raison d'etre*. That's typically augmented by statements of general operating standards that spell out the minimum requirements of behavior required for responsible corporate citizenship.

Consumer reports is no exception. My respect and admiration for the company is founded on statements like these from its website, its annual report and its monthly magazine:

• Its mission statement positions the organization as *"a reliable source of information consumers can depend on to help them distinguish hype from fact."*

- Its "No Commercial Use" policy *"helps ensure that we avoid even the appearance of endorsing a particular product or service for financial gain."*

- In its 2011 Annual Report Jim Guest, its President, stated, *"Everything we do is characterized by an unrivaled independence and scientific rigor, which together ensure we tell the truth each and every time."*

- In the December 2013 issue of Consumer Reports magazine he wrote, *"Consumer Reports believes that the more good information you have, the less you'll pay."*

As a non-profit corporation, Consumer Reports' revenue has traditionally come from (1) individuals who subscribe to its publications, purchase its New Car Price Service and make charitable gifts, and (2) "generous foundations and institutional grantors."

The organization has a substantial additional revenue source today. In 2011 Consumer Reports made TrueCar.com the information supplier and website manager for its popular New Car Price Service. That liaison also made TrueCar's dealers the ones CR sends consumers to in its "Build & Buy" program.

Auto dealers pay TrueCar.com $299 for every referral that leads to a sale. And, as Consumer Reports states on its website, *"Consumers Union collects a fee from TrueCar for vehicles purchased from a TrueCar Dealer."* My guess: about half of that $299. That's what I'd pay for sales that cost relatively little to generate.

In effect, that makes Consumer Reports another "third-party lead generator," accepting revenue that comes from new-car dealers. Which raises the question of the glaring inconsistency between its financial relationship with TrueCar and its claim that *"we avoid even the appearance of endorsing a particular product or service for financial gain."*

TrueCar's True Background

Founded in 2005, TrueCar provides pricing information and local price quotes from "certified" dealers in its "network." The company's trademark claim is "pricing transparency," defined primarily as "what others have paid for the same car."

Initially, its founder's take on the car business seemed much like mine, which is: "Every new car is a commodity — the same vehicle with the same price structure at every dealership selling that brand. Price is the only significant difference, and you'll always get the best price on any commodity by making suppliers compete for your business."

Like mine, his objective seemed to be to help consumers get the best price available without walking into a car store. He established a dealer network that provided competitive price bids to TrueCar users and paid TrueCar a fee for each sale made.

Unfortunately, there was a fatal flaw in his business model that ended up biting him you-know-where. His objective was to empower consumers, but his revenue came from dealers, and he made them madder than a mosquito trapped in a mannequin warehouse by publishing the lowest price in each market as a benchmark for other dealers to beat. That triggered "a race to the bottom," threatening dealer profitability broadly.

The predictable result: Over half of TrueCar's 5,700-dealer network bailed out, and TrueCar lost over $30 million. Perhaps remembering that Henry Ford said, "The only real mistake is one from which we learn nothing," TrueCar did a "180," creating an alternative business model that turned dealers into its profitable partners.

As I understand it, the company redefined its mission as *"bringing consumers and dealers together in a way that's good for both."* To avoid creating a Walmart-like image, it stopped featuring low prices as a major benefit.

That did the trick. Today over 6,000 dealers populate TrueCar's rebuilt dealer network. (In January 2014 there were 31,464 new-vehicle franchises in the U.S., so about 20% were TrueCar dealers.)

That's the TrueCar I see Consumer Reports partnering with today — a company dedicated to helping dealers profit by convincing consumers that they're getting a fair, no-hassle deal — *not* a company dedicated to helping consumers get the best price. (That was TrueCar's previous approach, the one that that cost the company $30 million.)

*　　*　　*　　*

Do the key auto-info websites know the truth about the industry's "redesign" of the automaker-dealer financial relationship? Yes, several of the largest do. I presented that evidence to them in . . . .

THE USA TODAY ROUNDTABLE MEETING

As noted earlier, I was in that November 2012 USA TODAY "open and candid, on-the-record" discussion on the question of *"whether online car shopping and information services are believable and are relevant in today's market."*

The other five participants were industry heavyweights: the President of AutoTrader, owner of Kelley Blue Book; Edmunds' Senior Director of Industry Analysis; TrueCar's Executive Vice President, Industry Solutions; the Editor-In-Chief at Cars.com; and the Director of Auto Testing at Consumer Reports, who is also involved with CR's pricing data. (Think of that gathering as little David vs. five Goliaths.)

As noted in Chapter 1, the newspaper's December 7, 2012 article on that roundtable discussion seemed to echo my conclusion. The subheading in the print edition was "No.1: Don't trust that invoice price."

At the meeting I passed out "The Exhibit" that starts on page 72. It illustrates for 47 popular models of 23 brands how the visible gross profit built into new-car pricing has been cut dramatically from its pre-Internet level in a deliberate, step-by-step process to hide a big cache of profit dollars in the invoice price that goes back to dealers in hidden, "below-the-line" incentive programs like those in Chapter 7.

You could have heard a pin drop as those auto-info honchos read it. It seemed to me that they'd never seen those numbers before. No one disputed them. No one said, "We've known that." Yet all those companies have been providing consumers with invoice prices for years. Some have for decades. (Note: A moonlighting court reporter recorded every word uttered in that meeting for the newspaper's later use in writing the article.)

One participant said the exhibit showed that the industry had responded to the publishing of invoice pricing online by saying, "*We need to find another way to mask what (dealers) are being paid so that people don't feel like they're getting screwed.*" No one disagreed.

Another added that there are sales incentive programs in which dealers will sell cars for thousands less than they'd normally charge to reach specific bonus targets. No one disagreed.

I challenged their "*pay what others paid*" recommendations with, "*You're treating consumers like they're idiots. Why would anyone pay close to an average price, when, by definition, it means that about half the people got a better price — maybe a much better price?*"

The reply I got was, "*Overwhelmingly, our market research shows that consumers ultimately don't want the best price. They just want a fair price.*" (No one disagreed.) Another participant said that a fair price "*means that when I tell my neighbor what I paid for the car, I won't be embarrassed.*" (No one disagreed.)

Does that statement accurately describe your objective when you buy a new car?

Another executive echoed that research claim, saying, *"We have data to support exactly what he said. We do post-purchase surveys of 100% of our consumers, and the ones who pay the least are the most dissatisfied. The ones who pay average or above average are actually more satisfied. Those who don't haggle over the last dollar spend an average of one or two hours less at the dealership. They feel they got treated fairly on the price and on the financing and trade-in values."*

On one level, that research has the ring of truth. Most people probably believe that to get the best price, they must walk into car store after car store and spend an hour or two haggling in each one. If that were true, I wouldn't want the best price, either.

Another participant played down the importance to consumers of the invoice price, saying that, true or false, it was *"just another data point"* among several that can be helpful and critical as shopping tools. That's certainly at loggerheads with what I've heard in conversations with tens of thousands of shoppers. Don't most consumers view all those websites primarily as "new-car pricing" sources?

As noted in Chapter 5, all those organizations use the vehicle's sticker price (that almost nobody pays) as the basis for their claims of consumers' "dollar savings" resulting from the use of their buying services. They defended that practice with, *"The states won't let us make any other price comparison."* (That's true in several states where dealers have lobbied their politicians to pass laws prohibiting comparisons with the invoice price in advertising.)

I had some fun with that response, saying, *"So the states make you use those padded savings numbers! You're saying 'the Devil makes you do it,' right? That straw man is loaded with more hay than Ray Bolger had as the scarecrow in 'The Wizard of Oz' movie!"*

There was no response. Unfortunately, many consumers don't see that exaggerated claim for what it is: pure hype.

Excluding a small number of vehicles that are close to impossible to deal on and totally redesigned cars in their initial few months on the market, when demand often exceeds supply, dealers will make below-MSRP offers to any walk-in with enough breath left to fog a mirror.

Some of those sites also include rebates and other incentive cash in their advertised "savings" claims. (That misleading practice is also covered in Chapter 5.)

Here's how I think you should interpret the real message behind what those participants were saying: *"If you want the lowest price, don't expect to get it by using our service. We'll help you get a 'fair' price and make the process hasssle-free."*

If you don't care about getting the best price, Edmunds, Kelley Blue Book, TrueCar/Consumer Reports, Cars.com and others are performing a useful public service. Just remember that they're sending you only to dealers in their "networks," who provide a major chunk of their total revenue — which, of course, comes out of your pocket. And those dealers know that you've been preconditioned by those sites to expect the dealer-friendly "fair" target prices those sites recommend to you.

But the stated objective of that roundtable meeting was to discuss the question of *"whether online car shopping and information services are believable and are relevant in today's market."* That should have been the crux of that discussion. The automaker-dealer financial relationship had undergone a dramatic, wide-reaching change that casts doubt upon the value of the invoice-based foundation for much of the information and advice those participants are providing to consumers. But it's an issue that wasn't addressed directly after they had the clear evidence of that revolution in their hands. I believe they all understood the implication of that exhibit and didn't want to discuss how it might affect their credibility. It was a cordial gathering, and I'd already become the one USA TODAY characterized as the meeting's "peppery contrarian." I'd heard what I read as a clear "unspoken message," and there was no need to belabor the obvious.

"Transparency" is a word you'll find on a few of those sites. They typically define it as *"the price others have actually paid for the same car in your market."*

My definition of transparency on this subject is a little different. It's *"characterized by visibility or accessibility of information about business practices."* And the central "business practice" the consumer needs to know to negotiate the best deals is the industry's total reconstruction of the automaker-dealer financial relationship that has turned the dealer invoice price into a misleading, overweight pretender.

Have any of those organizations revealed this game-changing fact to you since that November 2012 meeting? I haven't seen that happen, and I'm not holding my breath waiting.

Do you think it's just a coincidence that all five of them get substantial revenue from the auto industry? And that a smart dog doesn't bite the hand that feeds it?

I don't.

I believe the controlling reason for their silence is that telling the truth about the long-term, ongoing revolution in new-car pricing would jeopardize their revenue stream from the automobile business.

Indeed, for all those organizations, on this subject, it appears that $ilence is truly golden.

I'd looked forward to meeting the Consumer Reports representative in that roundtable discussion. Maybe I was naive, but I wanted to convey this important new fact (a.k.a the whole truth) to the organization whose President stated, *"Everything we do is characterized by an unrivaled independence and scientific rigor, which together ensure we tell the truth each and every time."*

After the meeting I asked CR's attendee for the name of the person responsible for their New Car Price Service, so that I could send him or her "The Exhibit." He pointedly ignored my request, and I sensed indignation in his demeanor. In essence, he dismissed the relevance of a fundamental truth directly connected to CR's signature product category — new cars — the consumer's second most expensive purchase. But like the other four participants, he left the meeting with that exhibit in his briefcase.

Consumer Reports is the only one of the five organizations in that discussion that actually *sells* consumers new-car pricing data and makes "target pricing" recommendations importantly based on that data. Yet a CR representative, apparently one with some involvement with its New Car Price Service, clearly didn't want me to convey the whole truth about new-car pricing to the person running that service.

Think about that for 30 seconds. A senior Consumer Reports executive, attending a meeting on *"whether online car shopping and information services are believable and are relevant in today's market,"* stonewalled my attempt to convey that pivotal fact about new car pricing — one that no attendee had disputed — to the people responsible for the brand's New Car Price Service. What does that say about his organization's proudly-heralded *"unrivaled independence and scientific rigor, which together ensure we tell the truth each and every time?"*

Isn't it interesting that all the other roundtable participants have access to the same pricing, holdback and incentive information as Consumer Reports, but not one of them — not even TrueCar, CR's financial partner — claims the ability to reveal the dealer's true cost? My guess: they have employees who have actually worked in the car business and understand that that's "intelligence" that even the CIA couldn't uncover.

I respect and appreciate Consumer Reports' diligent, insightful testing of the products and services we buy. And I think all the new-car buying services on the Internet, including that of Consumer Reports, are providing a useful public service for people who fit their research profile: consumers who *"ultimately don't want the best price. They just want a fair price."*

But this is not a product category in which "one size fits all." I've spent 20+ years dealing with over 125,000 smart, educated consumers whose objective is to get the best price available. And, knowing the truth, they approach the negotiating process with confidence and a plan for getting that price.

I'm not presenting here a wild-eyed *theory* about something that *might* have happened in the new-car business. I'm laying out the naked truth about a pricing revolution that's been going on for over 18 years. It's a crucial fact that every new-vehicle shopper deserves to know — a fact they're not getting from the sources they've trusted for years.

No industry "deep throat" fed me that data in "The Exhibit." It's all public information that was published, year in and year out, in cheap paperbacks that any curious human can still find on the Internet. I've combined it with what I've learned in almost two decades from over 125,000 "shallow-throated," car-shopping consumers to uncover and reveal what it says and what it means.

How is it possible that a 78-year-old man, working essentially alone, has been paying more attention to the car business than all those auto-industry information sources with lots of employees? Every one of them is up to its ears in new-car pricing information, day after day. That revolution has been happening in their information "wheelhouse" for almost two decades, but apparently gone either unnoticed. . . . . or unreported. (George Orwell wrote, "To see what is in front of one's nose needs a constant struggle.")

In my view, there are only two possible explanations for this, and if I were one of those sources, I wouldn't be proud of either one.

1. Like Rip Van Winkle, they've slept very soundly for over 18 years and missed it — an astounding oversight. Or . . . .

2. They've recognized that elephant that's been growing continually in their living room, but have chosen to ignore it. (Upton Sinclair wrote, *"It is difficult to get a man to understand something when his salary depends on his not understanding it."*)

What Charles Darwin said about the species is just as true about corporate organizations. *"It is not the strongest nor the most intelligent that survives, but the one that is most adaptable to change."*

We live in a fast-changing world. It's a brutal time for brands that don't maintain their relevance by reinventing themselves regularly as concrete new facts emerge that dramatically change the paradigm of the product or service category they deal with. (Paradigm: a theory or group of ideas about how something should be done or thought about.)

To the consumer, reality matters. Honesty matters. Facts matter. The whole truth matters. Behavior consistent with your principles matters.

In my view, there is no middle ground between today's truth and yesterday's, between what is and what used to be.

I don't believe any consumer information source can remain credible if the information it's providing is mired in yesterday's conventional wisdom and void of the current relevance consumers need and expect.

*   *   *   *

If you want a competent, reliable third party to conduct a bona fide competitive bidding process in your market for the car you want, consider using CarBargains, a national service of the nonprofit Consumers Checkbook. You can find the details and cost of the service at this website:checkbook.org/auto/carbarg.cfm. They're located in Washington, D.C. Phone: 800-475-7283.

I've known these scrupulously honest people over 20 years. (They accept no money from the dealers who win your business.) They are the folks I recommend to Fighting Chance customers who don't want to or can't do it themselves. (I don't accept money for those referrals.)

If you decide to use CarBargains, contact them well in advance of your need. That popular service often has a significant order backlog.

*   *   *   *

> **"Tell the truth, or someone will tell it for you."**
> — **Stephanie Klein**

On average, over 30,000 American consumers buy or lease a new vehicle every day. I believe they all deserve to know the truth — the whole truth.

If any organization I've pictured here as less-than-truthful about the sea change in new-car pricing and how it impacts consumers would like to challenge me in a national media forum, I'd relish the opportunity to put its credibility front-and-center in the public eye. (I'd start with an updated version of "The Exhibit" and describe what it says and what it means.) I believe CNN would love to host that debate.

On this subject, the horse called The Whole Truth has left the barn, and it's not going back.

Now, readers, prepare for a little attitude adjustment.

"I have experienced many instances of being obliged, by better information or fuller consideration, to change opinions that I once thought right but found to be otherwise."

— Benjamin Franklin

12

The dealer is not your enemy.

For decades the consumer approval rating of car dealers was down with those of lawyers and politicians. One wag coined the line, "99% of car dealers give the rest a bad name."

That long-standing poor reputation has improved dramatically in recent years. One of the major reasons is that car buyers now get post-purchase questionnaires asking them to rate several aspects of their dealer experience. As noted in earlier chapters, a bad "report card" can sucker punch a dealership in its most vulnerable body part — its bank balance.

There used to be all kinds of "dealer scams" consumers needed to guard against, but I'm convinced that the incidence of dealers pulling dishonest tricks today is very small compared to 10 or 15 years ago.

Fighting Chance's customers tend to be bright, educated people who can tell a rat from a hamster with their eyes closed. I've talked to tens of thousands of them. They describe their dealership experiences to me in detail, and in 20 years less than ten have reported attempted "scams." All were in one of two relatively minor categories that cost them time, but not money: (1) when they arrived at the dealership to finalize the deal, they learned the car had been sold to a higher bidder; or (2) a dealer claiming to have the car they wanted didn't have it and tried to sell them a more expensive model.

When you know your stuff, you don't get scammed.

Today all dealers want you to drive away a happy camper. They need the highest marks on their report cards, and they want you to refer everyone you know to their stores. They're not stupid. They know those things won't happen if they try to "scam" you.

In addition, consumers are getting smarter about the car-buying process. (I hope this book will accelerate that process a tad.)

As legendary UCLA basketball coach John Wooden warned, "Failing to prepare is preparing to fail." If you're well informed, you'll be in control of the negotiating process, and the dealers you contact will treat you with respect. Some may even say, "Are you sure you haven't been in the car business? You know so much about it."

I realize that some folks reading this and learning the game changing, jaw-dropping fact about the business that's been hidden from them for more than 15 years might be angry, feeling they've been cheated or lied to over those years. That the auto industry has deprived them of their birth-given right to know what every dealer ends up paying for a new car.

To them I say, "Grow up and get over it!" Where is it written that you have the right to that information for new cars, when you can't get it for any of the hundreds of other things you buy? Instead of feeling cheated or angry, maybe you should look in the mirror at the doofus who bought into the preposterous claim that someone can and will tell you what any retail store pays for any product it sells.

How could any serious, thinking person believe dealers could run a profitable business on the meager markup on the cost-of-goods-sold built into the published invoice and retail numbers?

You might think car dealers are making a killing, now that the invoice prices aren't the real McCoy anymore. That they're laughing all the way to bank with the big bucks they make on your deal, the bucks you can't find out about. Hold that thought while we examine a few more facts.

In the typical dealership, new-car sales account for 55% to 60% of total revenue. Used-vehicle sales represent 25% to 30%, and service and parts sales make up the other 10% to 20%.

How much pre-tax profit do you think stores earn on their total yearly revenue (total sales minus total expenses)? 5%? 10%? 15%? 20%? More?

Wrong.

In 2011 the average dealership had total sales of about $34 million and earned about a $786,000 net pre-tax profit. That was just 2.3% of sales, but it was the highest net profit level recorded since 1978!

Think about that. A net pre-tax profit of 2.3% of sales was the industry's best financial performance in over 30 years. They're not laughing all the way to the bank; the bank's laughing at them!

If any major national retail chain registered a net pre-tax profit that low, its entire management team would be sent to a North Korean labor camp in a Pyongyang minute.

As you surely know by now, I am a seeker and purveyor of truth. So cut those auto dealers a little slack. They're not lawyers or politicians. They're men and women with a significant percentage of their net worth at risk every day. And given all the competition, both between and within brands, it's not an easy business to run profitably.

They are not your enemy. They're just trying to make a living, like you are.

New-car shoppers who know what they're doing don't get ripped off. If you do your homework and approach dealers professionally, you'll find they will treat you with respect and appreciate the opportunity to win your business. And it's to your advantage to treat them the same way.

"In life, they shuffle the cards again every day. If we're paying attention, we should learn something from each day's deal that we can use to our benefit thereafter."

— James Bragg

12

The cards have been dealt.

When a big mountain of anecdotal information and indisputable, cold, hard facts leads to a conclusion that dramatically changes how we think about a subject, that process typically begs us to re-examine the way we've approached that subject in the past and to ask ourselves whether there's a better alternative.

You've been through a curious detective's "cold case" investigation of a turning point in the automaker-dealer financial relationship, a process that began in the 1990s and has continued, year after year, ever since. Its findings speak the truth loudly and clearly. The question is, "What does it mean, in terms of the actions you should take to use what it says to your benefit?" What should you actually do and not do, in concrete terms?

Fasten your seat belts. Here we go.

• Ignore the advice from any website that recommends one or more "target prices," then sends you to a small number of dealers in its "network" who reward it nicely when you buy — with dollars that come from your pocket. Those "targets" are prices that will never make their dealers unhappy. They're typically based on "average" transaction prices reported in your market area. (A few may list some lower prices as "great.")

Sites recommending a target price tend to present that number to you as if it were a revelation equivalent to the disclosure of Coke's secret syrup formula or the combination to the lock on Fort Knox. But don't look on that number as the "right" price just because the average clueless car shopper paid it, or close to it. Remember that "average" means that about half of the deals were better, and some were much better.

If I were a dealer in one of those "networks" and consumers called to say they were coming over to buy at those "target prices," I'd send chauffeur-driven limousines for them to make sure they didn't stop at another dealership on the way.

Will someone please explain how knowing what other people have paid for a car gives you an iota of leverage in a negotiation?

If I walked into a car store and said, "I know what other people have paid for that car, and I won't pay a penny more," what dealer in his right mind wouldn't be on me like a hobo on a baloney sandwich? I'll say it again: That's not a negotiation; it's a capitulation! (The definition of negotiation is "discussion aimed at reaching an agreement.")

You're not one of those "other people," you're *you*! And if you're reading this book, you're not one of the gullible penguins in those big auto-site colonies, believing everything you're told.

• <u>Your goal should be to get the best price available for the car you want in the area you live in at the time you're car shopping</u>. And that will never happen if you're aiming for a specific price, or even have a "right price" in mind.

With all that hidden, "below-the-line" cash floating around in the automobile marketplace, it's fiscal insanity to fixate on any "target" or "right" price, no matter how it's figured. When you do that, you set an automatic floor under your potential transaction price. How do you know it couldn't be lower, maybe by a lot?

• <u>Understand that you're not shopping for a Renoir or the Mona Lisa, you're shopping for a commodity</u>. I learned that in 1997, when a Colorado Springs customer was shopping for a $16,000 to $18,000 midsize sedan. He contacted 12 dealers, asking for price proposals. He said, "It was like rolling a bottle of wine into a jail cell full of drunks." There was over a $1,000 difference between the low and high bids.

A light bulb started blinking in my challenged brain, shouting, "Of course! The car you want, configured the way you want it, is the same car with the same price structure at every franchised dealer for that brand. It's a commodity. And you'll always get the best price on any commodity by making the suppliers compete."

This has always been true in the car business. It's more true now than ever, given the totally "redesigned" automaker-dealer financial relationship that puts the dealers' focus on hidden sales targets that deliver big-bucks bonus checks.

The corollary is that, if one's objective is to get the best price available, you'll almost never accomplish that by (a) walking into a car store to negotiate, (b) making an offer, or (c) limiting yourself to any auto-info website's "dealer network."

But millions of people still do. Eventually we all stop waiting up to see the Easter Bunny, but most folks still believe that ancient fairy tale about "dealer cost" and the "right way to buy a new car."

• <u>You'll get the best price by making several dealers compete for your business.</u> Like Fighting Chance customers, you'll do that by contacting dealers that *you* choose from your home or office and getting six to ten of them to agree to give you a competitive price proposal.

Two, three or four participants doesn't cut it. Given all the "below-the-line" incentive programs you now know are everywhere in the business, you need to involve more dealers to improve your chance of hitting one that's close to a sales target that's attached to a big check. In today's fluid incentive environment, the dealer who's the low bidder this month might be the high bidder two or three months later.

• <u>It's OK if a few participants are 50 or more miles away.</u> A more remote dealer might see you as business he'd never get otherwise and sell at a better price than he'd offer his local prospects, saving you more than enough money to make that trip worthwhile.

• <u>You don't have to get the car serviced where you buy it.</u> Folks are moving into your town every year with cars they bought somewhere else, and dealers for those makes are delighted to get their service business. The parts and service manager's paycheck is based on the revenue generated in that department, not on sales.

• <u>The best deals usually come near the end of every month.</u> Dealer owners typically come from sales, not service. They've got monthly targets, even when there are no hidden cash programs ending then. They're trying to beat last month, or the same month last year, and they want to pick their "salesperson of the month." So late-month is always the best time to solicit competitive bids.

Why aren't Consumer Reports and the other auto-pricing websites telling you that? Because the network dealers who provide their revenue want to keep their sales churning every day, not just at month-end, when they're typically willing to deal more aggressively to meet targets.

• <u>Most important: You need to take personal control of the purchase process.</u> It's your money that's at stake – a lot of your money. Don't cede power over it to a "middleman" that's another mouth you must feed.

Let's assume you "click thru" for a quote from a dealer in an auto website's network, but I contact that same dealer directly. We're shopping for identical vehicles. Who will get the lowest price proposal?

You can bet that I will. Why? Because (a) he doesn't have to pay any "middleman" site for sending me to him, and (b) he knows that you entered the process with a very modest expectation about the price you'll get, based on the dealer-friendly target prices those auto sites publish, and that his competition is just a few other "network" dealers who know that, too.

By contrast, I've made it clear that he's just one of an undefined number of dealers I'm contacting, so he knows he'll need to sharpen his pencil and quote a better price to win my business. I've also made myself a much more real prospect because I've actually talked to him to get his agreement to participate.

*   *   *   *

Now that you know the whole truth, shouldn't your objective be to get the best price available for the car you want?

I think I just heard the bell ring.

Class dismissed.

But the teacher would like you to do a little homework, so please read the last few pages.

"A lie can travel halfway around the world while the truth is putting on its shoes."

— Charles Spurgeon

Epilogue

Twelve to thirteen million consumers buy or lease a new vehicle in this country every year. My mission is to help make them more knowledgeable about that process. Understanding the whole truth about the automaker-dealer financial relationship is critical to their navigating that journey successfully — especially when the information they're getting about that relationship on the Internet has been obsolete for over 18 years. This book is the sole source of that truth in print — at least it is as I'm typing this in the first quarter of 2014.

If you feel enlightened and empowered by what you've read, and if you agree that this is something every car-shopping consumer should know, I hope you'll consider helping to make "Letting The Cat Out Of The Bag" more visible on the Internet as a must-read for every potential new-car buyer.

I can't do this alone. I need you to help spread the word to everyone you know, friend or foe, via your email contacts and social networks (Facebook, Twitter, etc.), so that they can spread it to everyone they know.

If you have media contacts you think might be interested in this revelation, please mention the book to them. It's available in both paperback and ebook formats.

If you're so inclined, I also encourage you to go to Amazon to write a glowing (or at least semi-glowing) review.

You're among a small number of people in the vanguard of a new way of thinking about car shopping, based on solid, game-changing facts that it took over 15 years to uncover completely.

So the next time someone approaches you wearing a "Got Truth?" t-shirt, you can proudly respond, "Yup. It's a book called 'Letting The Cat Out Of The Bag.' If you're thinking about buying a new car, you need to get it."

I appreciate the time you've taken to peel this onion with me. I hope you feel that finally, someone's told you the whole truth about the new-car business.

I also hope I've made you smile occasionally along the way. Because the time you spend smiling and laughing is not deducted from your total life span. It's a little "overtime" period we all get.

Ciao for now,

James Bragg

"The Exhibit"

• On November 27, 2012, I presented the information that starts on the next page to senior executives of Kelley Blue Book, Cars.com, TrueCar, Edmunds and Consumer Reports in an open and candid, on-the-record USA TODAY roundtable discussion on "whether online car-shopping and information services are believable and are relevant in today's market."

• Using 47 popular models of 23 different auto brands, the exhibit shows dramatically how the industry has cleverly disguised dealer-incentive dollars as dealer-cost dollars by steadily increasing the invoice price by more than the MSRP for over 18 years.

• When I distributed it to the participants, you could have heard a pin drop in that room. My startling conclusion was that no one there was aware of that game-changing fact.

• If I were in their shoes, I would have left the meeting concerned that, if that fact were widely known, consumers would see that the information and advice I'd been providing was built on a foundation that crumbled over a decade ago.

James Bragg

% Markup Built Into The Sticker Price
(MSRP − Invoice Price ÷ MSRP = % Markup/Gross Profit)

Acura TL Sedan
1994	15.2%
1996	13.2%
1998	10.7%
2000	9.8%
2003	8.8%
2007	8.3%
2008	8.1%
2011	7.2%
2013	6.4%

Acura TSX Sedan
1994	14.1%
1996	12.1%
1998	10.7%
2000	9.8%
2004	8.8%
2007	8.2%
2008	8.0%
2011	7.0%
2013	6.2%

Audi A4 Sedan
1993	15.2%
1995	12.1%
2000	11.1%
2002	9.1%
2007	7.4%
2013	7.1%

Audi A4 Avant/AllRoad

1993	16.4%
1998	11.5%
2000	10.6%
2002	9.2%
2007	7.4%

BMW 3-Series Convertible

1993	16.3%
1995	15.9%
1996	13.6%
1998	12.4%
2000	9.5%
2002	8.6%
2013	8.0%

BMW 5-Series Sedan

1993	16.2%
1998	12.4%
2000	9.7%
2002	8.7%
2013	8.0%

BMW 7-Series Sedan

1993	18.2%
1996	13.9%
1998	12.5%
2000	9.8%
2002	8.7%
2013	8.0%

Buick LaCrosse

1993	12.5%
1995	10.5%
2000	8.5%
2007	5.5%
2013	4.0%

Buick Regal

1993	12.5%
1996	8.5%
2013	4.0%

Cadillac DTS/XTS

1993	13.5%
1995	8.5%
2000	8.2%
2007	6.5%
2013	5.5%

Chevrolet Corvette

1993	14.5%
1998	12.5%
2007	10.5%
2013	6.5%

Chevrolet Impala

1993	12.5%
1995	9.5%
1998	8.5%
2007	5.5%
2013	4.0%

Chrysler 300

Year	Percent
1993	12.7%
1995	10.0%
2000	8.8%
2003	8.3%
2005	7.4%
2007	7.0%
2011	5.0%
2013	4.6%

Chrysler Town & Country

Year	Percent
1993	10.4%
1994	9.6%
2002	8.9%
2011	6.0%
2013	5.2%

Dodge Charger

Year	Percent
1993	12.9%
1995	10.1%
1998	8.7%
2004	7.5%
2007	6.9%
2013	4.5%

Dodge Grand Caravan

Year	Percent
1994	10.0%
2002	9.0%
2005	8.5%
2011	5.4%
2013	4.8%

Ford Explorer

Year	Percent
1993	11.4%
1996	10.3%
2003	9.6%
2008	7.2%
2011	7.0%
2013	6.8%

Ford Mustang

Year	Percent
1993	10.4%
1995	10.0%
1996	9.1%
2002	8.5%
2011	8.1%
2013	7.7%

Honda Accord

Year	Percent
1993	16.0%
1995	11.6%
2000	11.1%
2002	10.0%
2011	9.4%
2012	8.6%
2013	8.5%

Honda Civic

Year	Percent
1993	15.0%
1995	10.3%
2000	9.7%
2002	8.6%
2011	8.0%
2013	7.1%

Hyundai Accent
1993	9.8%
1998	7.4%
2000	6.4%
2013	2.9%

Hyundai Elantra
1993	11.7%
1998	10.4%
2000	8.0%
2007	7.5%
2013	4.2%

Hyundai Sonata
1993	12.3%
1998	11.9%
2000	10.8%
2002	9.8%
2013	6.5%

Infiniti G Sedan
1993	20.0%
1995	16.0%
1996	15.2%
2003	9.4%
2007	8.0%
2011	7.7%
2013	7.4%

Jaguar XJ Sedan

Year	Percent
1995	18.4%
1996	15.9%
1998	12.6%
2007	8.9%
2013	8.0%

Jeep Grand Cherokee

Year	Percent
1993	9.9%
2002	8.8%
2011	6.0%
2013	5.1%

Jeep Wrangler 2-door

Year	Percent
1993	9.1%
2007	8.8%
2011	5.9%
2013	5.8%

Lexus ES Sedan

Year	Percent
1994	18.0%
1995	17.0%
1996	15.0%
1998	13.1%
2002	11.3%
2008	10.3%
2011	9.3%
2013	6.3%

Lexus GS Sedan

Year	Value
1994	18.0%
1995	17.0%
1996	15.0%
1998	14.1%
2007	13.0%
2008	12.0%
2011	11.0%
2013	7.0%

Lexus LS Sedan

Year	Value
1994	20.0%
1995	18.0%
1996	16.0%
1998	15.2%
2002	13.0%
2008	12.0%
2011	11.0%
2013	8.0%

Lexus RX SUV

Year	Value
2000	13.1%
2002	12.0%
2004	11.5%
2011	9.5%
2012	6.5%

Lincoln Town Car

Year	Value
1993	15.3%
1995	13.0%
1996	12.0%
1998	9.0%
2003	8.6%
2011	6.2%

Mazda3 Sedan
1993	9.9%
1995	8.9%
2000	7.5%
2011	6.4%
2013	4.4%

Mazda6 Sedan
1993	12.9%
1995	10.9%
1998	10.0%
2000	8.8%
2002	7.8%
2011	7.6%
2013	5.6%

Mercedes C-Class Sedan
1993	17.0%
1995	15.0%
1998	13.0%
2000 to 2013	7.0%

Mercedes E-Class Sedan
1993	17.0%.
1996	13.0%
2000 to 2013	7.0%

Nissan Maxima
1993	13.3%
1995	12.5%
1996	11.0%
2000	10.1%
2004	8.6%
2013	8.4%

Nissan Sentra

1993	11.8%
1995	10.8%
1996	9.4%
2000	8.6%
2013	6.7%

Subaru Legacy Sedan

1993	12.1%
1995	10.5%
2000	9.4%
2007	7.2%
2011	6.8%
2013	6.2%

Subaru Outback Wagon

1993	12.1%
1995	10.5%
2000	9.4%
2007	7.2%
2013	6.4%

Toyota Camry

1993	16.0%
1995	13.3%
1998	12.5%
2002	11.0%
2008	10.8%
2013	9.0%

Toyota Corolla

1993	14.0%
1995	12.3%
1998	11.4%
2003	9.5%
2013	7.3%

Toyota 4Runner

1993	15.5%
1996	13.2%
1998	12.5%
2003	10.7%
2008	9.7%
2013	8.0%

VW Jetta Sedan

1994	9.6%
1995	7.7%
2000	9.0%
2002	8.8%
2007	6.6%
2008	5.4%
2013	4.0%

VW Passat

1993	11.8%
1995	10.0%
2000	8.1%
2007	7.3%
2008	6.4%
2013	4.1%

Volvo S80 Sedan

1994	14.0%
1995	9.5%
1996	8.6%
1998	8.4%
2000	8.2%
2002 to 2013	6.0%

Volvo XC 70

1994	13.6%
1995	9.1%
1996	8.3%
1998	8.1%
2000	7.4%
2013	4.1%

Words Truth Seekers Live By

"Facts do not cease to exist because they are ignored."
— Aldous Huxley

"You know a person is teaching the truth when no one debates it."
— Amunhotep El Bey

"If you tell the truth, you don't have to remember anything."
— Mark Twain

"The truth will set you free, but first it will piss you off."
— Gloria Steinem

"The truth does not change according to our ability to stomach it."
— Flannery O'Connor

"Rather than love, than money, than fame, give me truth."
— Henry David Thoreau

"Tell the truth, or someone will tell it for you."
— Stephanie Klein

"No persons are more frequently wrong, than those who will not admit they are wrong."
— Francois de La Rochefoucauld

"The past has no power over the present moment."
— Eckhart Tolle

"Three things can not hide for long: the Moon, the Sun and the Truth."
— Gautama Buddha

"All truth passes through three stages: First, it is ridiculed; Second, it is violently opposed; Third, it is accepted as self-evident."
— Arthur Schopenhauer

"There are two ways to be fooled. One is to believe what isn't true; the other is to refuse to believe what is true."
— Soren Kierkegaard

"Most men would rather deny a hard truth than face it."
— George R.R. Martin

"Man is always prey to his truths. Once he has admitted them, he cannot free himself from them."
— Albert Camus

"There comes a time when one must take the position that is neither safe nor politic nor popular, but he must do it because conscience tells him it is right."
— Martin Luther King, Jr.

"Truth is like the sun. You can shut it out for a time, but it ain't going away."
— Elvis Presley

"If someone is able to show me that what I think or do is not right, I will happily change, for I seek the truth, by which no one was ever truly harmed. It is the person who continues in his self-deception and ignorance who is harmed."
— Marcus Aurelius

"Time is precious, but truth is more precious than time."
— Benjamin Disraeli

"The high-minded man must care more for the truth than for what people think."
— Aristotle

"The ideals which have always shone before me and filled me with joy are goodness, beauty, and truth."
— Albert Einstein

"There is no greatness where there is not simplicity, goodness, and truth."
— Leo Tolstoy

"Lies run sprints, but the truth runs marathons."
— Michael Jackson

"The truth is always an insult or a joke, lies are generally tastier. We love them. The nature of lies is to please. Truth has no concern for anyone's comfort."
— Katherine Dunn

"To see what is in front of one's nose needs a constant struggle."
— George Orwell

"When truth is replaced by silence, the silence is a lie."
— Yevgeny Yevtushenko

"Trust starts with truth and ends with truth."
— Santosh Kalwar

"Truth would quickly cease to be stranger than fiction, once we got as used to it."
— H. L. Mencken

"You may choose to look the other way but you can never say again that you did not know."
— William Wilberforce

"You don't believe things because they make your life better, you believe them because they're true."
— Veronica Roth

"There are few reasons for telling the truth, but for lying the number is infinite."
— Carlos Ruiz Zafon

"The truth is messy. It's raw and uncomfortable. You can't blame people for preferring lies."
— Holly Black

"The truth may be puzzling. It may take some work to grapple with. It may be counterintuitive. It may contradict deeply held prejudices. It may not be consonant with what we desperately want to be true. But our preferences do not determine what's true."
— Carl Sagan

"When two opposite points of view are expressed with equal intensity, the truth does not necessarily lie exactly halfway between them. It is possible for one side to be simply wrong."
— Richard Dawkins

"Better a cruel truth than a comfortable delusion."
— Edward Abbey

"People often claim to hunger for truth, but seldom like the taste when it's served up."
— George R.R. Martin

"We don't get to chose what is true. We only get to choose what we do about it."
— Kami Garcia

"Being in a minority, even in a minority of one, did not make you mad. There was truth and there was untruth, and if you clung to the truth even against the whole world, you were not mad."
— George Orwell

"Either you repeat the same conventional doctrines everybody is saying, or else you say something true, and it will sound like it's from Neptune."
— Noam Chomsky

"What cannot be said above all must not be silenced but written."
— Jacques Derrida

"No human should mislead another by promising them something they know to be untrue."
— Santosh Kalwar

"In a room where people unanimously maintain a conspiracy of silence, one word of truth sounds like a pistol shot."
— Czeslaw Milosz

"It is perfectly monstrous,' he said, at last, 'the way people go about nowadays saying things against one behind one's back that are absolutely and entirely true."
— Oscar Wilde

"A truth that no one knows is still the truth."
— Sharon Shinn

"We are willing to believe anything other than the truth."
— Carlos Ruiz Zafon

"Convictions are more dangerous foes of truth than lies."
— Friedrich Nietzsche

"More people would learn from their mistakes if they weren't so busy denying them"
— Harold J. Smith

"I like the truth, even when it does trouble me."
— Juliet Marillier

"If you're not gonna tell the truth, then why start talking?"
— Gene Wilder

"Because even if the lie is beautiful, the truth is what you face in the end."
— Lauren DeStefano

"There are a dozen views about everything until you know the answer. Then there's never more than one."
— C.S. Lewis

"Because even though the truth can set you free, that doesn't mean it won't be painful."
— Ally Carter

"Why did adults have to be so thick? They always say "Tell the truth," and when you do, they don't believe you. What's the point?"
— Rick Riordan

"I don't think there's anything wrong with telling the truth. I know it isn't fashionable."
— Craig Ferguson

"It is not easy to keep silent when silence is a lie."
— Victor Hugo

"In all debates, let truth be thy aim, not victory, or an unjust interest."
— William Penn

"I'm not mean, I'm honest. Nobody is ever straightforward. But sometimes people need to hear the truth."
— Jessica Warman

"Proof is boring. Proof is tiresome. Proof is an irrelevance. People would far rather be handed an easy lie than search for a difficult truth, especially if it suits their own purposes."
— Joe Abercrombie

"What is important is not what you hear said, it's what you observe."
— Michael Connelly

"The truth is seldom welcome, especially at dinner."
— Margaret Atwood

"She was reflecting back on a truth she had learned over the years: that people heard what they wanted to hear, saw what they wanted, believed what they wanted."
— Jeffrey Deaver

"It is error only, and not truth, that shrinks from inquiry. "
— Thomas Paine

"Say what you have to say, not what you ought. Any truth is better than make-believe."
— Henry David Thoreau

"Integrity is a bugger, it really is. Lying can get you into difficulties, but to really wind up in the crappers try telling nothing but the truth."
— David Mitchell

"If it can be destroyed by the truth, it deserves to be destroyed by the truth."
— Carl Sagan

"The truth that makes men free is for the most part the truth which men prefer not to hear."
— Herbert Agar

"If you are unable to find the truth right where you are, where else do you expect to find it?"
— Dogen

"The best way to show that a stick is crooked is not to argue about it or to spend time denouncing it, but to lay a straight stick alongside it"
— D.L. Moody

"I was bold in the pursuit of knowledge, never fearing to follow truth and reason to whatever results they led."
— Thomas Jefferson

"It is discouraging how many people are shocked by honesty and so few by deceit"
— Noel Coward

"People who pride themselves on their 'complexity' and deride others for being 'simplistic' should realize that the truth is often not very complicated. What gets complex is evading the truth."
— Thomas Sowell

"Comfort is no test of truth. Truth is often far from being comfortable."
— Swami Vivekananda

"Belief means not wanting to know what is true."
— Friedrich Nietzsche

"One of the few things in life that cannot possibly do harm in the end is the honest pursuit of the truth."
— Peter Kreeft

"Your fear of the truth does not hide or dilute it."
— Steve Maraboli

"For people who say they hate being lied to, just start telling them nothing but the pure truth--about everything. That will teach them."
— Seth Adam Brown

"I don't pretend to know everything; I just only speak on matters I know I'll win."
— Criss Jami

"Never assume the obvious is true."
— William Safire

"Just because something isn't a lie does not mean that it isn't deceptive. A liar knows that he is a liar, but one who speaks mere portions of truth in order to deceive is a craftsman of destruction."
— Criss Jami

"Eliminate all other factors, and the one which remains must be the truth."
— Arthur Conan Doyle

"People trust their eyes above all else - but most people see what they wish to see, or what they believe they should see; not what is really there"
— Zoe Marriott

"Apparently people don't like the truth, but I do like it; I like it because it upsets a lot of people. If you show them enough times that their arguments are bullshit, then maybe just once, one of them will say, 'Oh! Wait a minute - I was wrong.' I live for that happening. Rare, I assure you"
— Lemmy Kilmister

"I would have offered you a forest of truth, but you wish to speak of a single leaf"
— David Gemmell

"The truth is sometimes a poor competitor in the market place of ideas – complicated, unsatisfying, full of dilemmas, always vulnerable to misinterpretation and abuse."
— George F. Kennan

"Discussion is impossible with someone who claims not to seek the truth, but already to possess it."
— Romaine Rolland

"The number of people who believe a thing has no bearing upon its truth."
— Marie Sexton

"The truth is like a lion; you don't have to defend it. Let it loose; it will defend itself."
— Augustine of Hippo

"I offer my opponents a bargain: if they will stop telling lies about us, I will stop telling the truth about them.
— Adlai E. Stevenson II

"You cannot believe everything you hear"
— Jude Morgan

"The truth doesn't mind being told every once in a while."
— Alysha Speer

"What you resist persists."
— Carl Jung

"To crooked eyes truth may wear a wry face"
— J.R.R. Tolkien

Half the truth is still a whole lie.
— Yiddish proverb

"The search for truth takes you where the evidence leads you, even if, at first, you don't want to go there."
— Bart D. Ehrman

"Men willingly believe what they wish."
— Julius Caesar

"I'm for truth, no matter who tells it."
— Malcolm X

"I didn't set out to discover Truth. I was simply hungry and digging deep in the back of the fridge and boom! There it was. And I've got to tell you, the Truth was tasty."
— Jarod Kintz

"It is almost impossible to carry the torch of truth through a crowd without singeing somebody's beard."
— Georg Christoph Lichtenberg

"I am not bound to win, but I am bound to be true. I am not bound to succeed, but I am bound to live up to what light I have."
— Abraham Lincoln

"If you would be a real seeker of truth, it is necessary that at least once in your life you doubt, as far as possible."
— René Descartes

"Of life's two chief prizes, beauty and truth, I found the first in a loving heart and the second in a laborer's hand."
— Kahlil Gibran

"Truth does not become more true by virtue of the fact that the entire world agrees with it, nor less so even if the whole world disagrees with it."
— Maimonides

"Don't worry about being effective. Just concentrate on being faithful to the truth."
— Dorothy Day

"Understanding is a three-edged sword: your side, their side and the truth."
— J. Michael Connelly

"Once you place the crown of liar on your head, you can take it off again, but it leaves a stain for all time."
— Terry Goodkind

9805692R10060

Made in the USA
San Bernardino, CA
28 March 2014